# THE RISE AND FALL OF OUR YOUTH

WELDON R. SHAW

LIBRARY TALES PUBLISHING

PRINTED IN THE UNITED STATES OF AMERICA

**Published by:**
Library Tales Publishing, Inc.
511 6th Avenue #56
New York, NY 10011
www.LibraryTalesPublishing.com

For general information on our other products and services, please contact our Customer Care Department at 1-800-754-5016, or fax 917-463-0892. For technical support, please visit www.LibraryTalesPublishing.com

Library Tales Publishing also publishes its books in a variety of electronic formats. Every content that appears in print is available in electronic books.

ISBN-13: 978-0692429211
ISBN-10: 0692429212

# TABLE OF CONTENTS

# AUTHOR INTRODUCTION

Hi, my name is Weldon Shaw. I was raised with old-fashioned philosophies by my Mother, who was a single parent. Society today appears to be overloaded with too many distractions and I do not like the path our children are going down. I have worked with troubled youth for 25 years as a Gang Investigator and Debriefer in the California Department of Corrections.

The one thing that has really bothered me and I am tired of seeing is youthful people wasting their lives behind bars. This has led to writing of *The Rise And Fall Of Our Youth*. This is a common sense approach to help parents to see the obstacles that may impact your children while growing up.

A Debriefer in the California Department of Corrections is a person who interviews and writes biographies of high-profile gang members who desire to drop out of their respective gangs.

Over the years I have interviewed hundreds of gang members and I always tried to take my interviews much further than they needed to go. With each opportunity I had to interview a criminal, I always made sure I asked the question of what made them go down the criminal path in life.

As an adult, I have tried to step back and take an outside view of people who I come into contact with on a daily basis. While observing people conducting their daily routines, I find myself analyzing their behavior, trying to determine what makes them act in the manner they do.

My wife will tell you I have a nasty habit of analyzing those around me. The first few minutes I spend

with a person will determine whether I will like them or not. It is a sense I was born with, an inner sense that was nurtured during my upbringing. It is an inner feeling I trust very much. It tells me if I have a good, moral person in my presence
or a troubled individual.

With that being said, I want you to understand one thing. No matter what a person's upbringing is, the path a person takes in life is solely determined by them. Yes, a bad upbringing makes the road of life harder, but ultimately the individual themselves decides what direction they are heading in life.

Let me tell you a little about my upbringing as a child To assure you, I had plenty of opportunities to go down the wrong road of life, just as many other people did. I was born in 1962 in Los Angeles, California, during the peace, love, sex, drugs and rock and roll era. I was raised by a single mom, not unlike so many kids are today, and I had three older brothers.

As a kid growing up, I do not remember much about my real father, because he was never around. When he did come around, he was like a stranger to me. My mother was a very loving woman. She worked herself into the ground, trying to make sure her kids had the things they needed while growing up. It was not unusual for her to work 16-hour shifts at the local tasty freeze just to keep the house running.

As a toddler my brothers were much older than me. The oldest being around 20, was serving his country in Vietnam. My mother worried about him day and night, like so many mothers did during the war. Many soldiers were coming back home in body bags and she feared for my brother's safety.

The next oldest brother was around 18 and was a very fun loving person, who had adapted pretty well without a father figure being in his life. The brother next to me was around 17 and did not fair as well. He had a lot of frustration built up in him because of the divorce situation. In the end he stayed under the influence of narcotics most of the time to escape the real world.

As everyone knows the '60s were all about drugs, sex and rock and roll. The drugs flowed freely during this time. It was a time of experimenting for the youth culture. My brothers at home were not much different than most kids during this time period. They experimented with narcotics and alcohol.

My mother had to work day and night, resulting in her being away from home and worrying about what we were up to. Her nerves were shot from having to work 16-hour days, but when she did get home, she made it a point to sit down with us to find out what we had been up to all day. She suffered from nerve-induced migraines for a very long time, but she always kept moving forward never giving up on her job as a parent.

While she was at work the parties were rampant at our house, with sometimes 50 teenagers there. Being it was the '60s there was every imaginable drug present, uppers, downers, speed, LSD, cocaine, reds and so forth. The alcohol of choice for teenagers back then was Valley High wine, Ripple, Mad Dog 20/20, Thunderbird and beer.

I observed fights taking place, tattooing and tons of profanity. The reason I am telling you all of this is I want to get it across to you as parents that each individual child chooses his or her own path to go down in life. It is your job to show them the right path, while giving them the best family life possible, and the most important thing, a lot of love. It is your child's job to take the right path that is shown to them.

While growing up in this type of environment I could have easily become consumed by drug use, like those who surrounded me. Instead I chose the right road in life and joined the military, and later I took on a career in law enforcement.

There have been many successful people raised in a bad family structure or environment. Yes, your environment can consume you, but it can also make you stronger and fuel you to want much more out of life.

When this type of person becomes an adult, it assists them in wanting more for their children.

I am not saying it is easy. However, the sky is the limit for each young adult. They just have to decide if they are going to be consumed by self pity and their environment or if they are going to fight and do something better for themselves.

I cannot give up on our kids. I cannot keep from thinking, if we as adults can get some of the old laws back in place, laws like those that give us the ability to raise our children and discipline them when needed, we might be able to save so many kids from the terrible existence of living within prison walls.

# ABOUT THE BOOK

During the last 25 years I have worked for the California Department of Corrections. Twelve of those years were spent as a Gang Investigator inside the prison walls and on the streets.

During my career as an investigator, I had the opportunity to interview hundreds of troubled young adults, which led to me writing over 3,000 documents. The documents outlined the individual's behavior, details about their upbringing, and safety issues inside the prison and on the streets. In the end the troubles they were facing came down to learned negative behavioral traits and bad decision making.

I also had special training in the area of being what they called a debriefer. As a debriefer, I wrote biographies of key gang members and their life histories. These individuals were seeking help to get out of the gang lifestyle.

I enjoyed having conversations with inmates from various cultural backgrounds. Inmates seemed to be very comfortable around me, and I had the ability to get them to open up to me and drop their war-beaten shield for a few moments of conversation.

I took full advantage of every moment I spent talking to these young adults, hoping to make an impact on their lives as well as gain valuable information in regards to what made them go wrong in life.

I ensured our conversations would lead to me getting into their heads for a few moments while their shield was down, leaving them with something to think about as they walked away.

This is not unlike raising your own children, make sure every conversation has a lesson to be learned, even if it is a small lesson. I walked those prison yards for 25 years and saw so many young adults whose lives were wasting away within those walls. Not unlike a family structure at home, there were times when I caught individuals doing wrong, and had to put a stop to what they were doing.

Most of them were starving for conversation and attention from what they saw as a role model type person. To them, a role model stood for the opposite of everything they did wrong in life. If you were the type of person who would talk to them about the world outside of prison, they would bend your ear all day long.

Once they gained confidence in me, they would eventually open up, talking to me about the bad things they experienced in life. If you gave them a little support and hope they could still turn their lives around. You could actually see their minds thinking about it, with a glimpse of hope in their eyes. In their environment, hope and a chance in life are not things they hear much about, and when they come around they usually fail to recognize them.

Now I just used the words confidence, hope and support. These are three basic things, you as a parent are supposed to be instilling into your own kids as you raise them. The confidence that you will always love them and be there for them when they need you most. The hope that they can be anything they want to be in life, and reassurance that destiny is right at their fingertips. The confidence that you will be there to support their decisions and guide them in the right direction when needed.

I have worked in some of the toughest environments imaginable, especially at Corcoran State Prison Security Housing Unit. This has been deemed by the media as one of the toughest prisons in the nation.

The personalities of inmates I met along the way ranged from the kid next door demeanor, to a psychotic personality, who was constantly trying to figure out how to get their hands around your throat to kill you. I have observed every imaginable bad behavior trait that has been written about by doctors. I have personally observed almost every mental disorder society has to offer from the serial killer, rapist, and child molester to the self mutilator.

Over the years while taking a wide view of society and watching other people in action, I have come up with a few areas of interest that I feel have impacted our youth in a negative manner. These areas of interest have had a very strong negative impact on society as a whole. I will go as far as to say they have even affected the manner you raise your children, resulting in a negative environment, altering a child's personality, mind and in some instances makes them mentally unstable.

I want to say this book is not a book about how best to raise your children, but rather a book to open your mind up and get you thinking. It should be considered a tool to be referred to. I do not feel there is a book written that I would put my full trust in to raise a child by. Raising a child is a personal tailored experience, in which you will instill part of yourself into your child.

All the subjects covered in this book could easily have a book dedicated to them alone. So in the end, I guess you can call this an overview of some of the most controversial issues that will impact your children's lives. I know as a person you will agree with some of the things I say and disagree with others, and that is OK. The biggest thing I want to accomplish is giving you something to think about and hopefully a foundation to start raising your child by.

It seems society has gradually fallen apart due to one bad decision after another made by politicians, local officials and lobby groups who have an agenda for personal gains. These bad decisions are politically motivated, religiously motivated, and financially motivated, and support is motivated by a particular theory or idea.

The bad decisions made over the years have left our country and states individually in massive debt, leaving our youth with the burden to pay it off later. The negative influence of media such as TV and video games over the years have led to the disintegration of our youth's morals. It has also painted a bleak future for our kids and has given them a sense of being lost.

A lot of this book is based on my own personal thoughts and observations; my personal feeling about how society has let our youth down resulting in incarceration and a sense that they have no future. It also talks about how corrupt our political system and legal system are, which has let all of us down so other individuals can receive personal gains.

Each of these areas of interest will become the headings for my chapters in this book. Like I said earlier, I am just an old-fashioned guy who is sharing his thoughts with you; the same thoughts a lot of you have had in the past. I want you to have the feeling we are just two people sitting at the kitchen table having a conversation about what is wrong with society.

As a parent I will say there is no such thing as a perfect family. No matter what your stature is in life, from being a doctor, politician, lawyer or just a common person, none of us are immune to the tragedies of life. We all have family issues and children that give us trouble. Some parenting issues are worse than those experienced by others.

The bottom line is, it all comes back to the home environment and the time you as a parent put into your children. You can live in the ghetto and produce great young adults, with a strong sense of right and wrong and ambition to do better for themselves.

You can be wealthy, giving your child everything money can buy, but fail to give them the one thing money cannot buy, and that is love and proper morals. The lack of a proper home environment can result in an uncontrollable young adult, whose parents are having to pay tons of money to keep them out of prison.

Read my thoughts I have taken the time to put down on paper. Understand that there is no perfect solution to raising a child. A lot of life is trial and error, but there are a few basics you need to instill in your children as they grow, such as values, morals and ethics. You need to understand there are other things that will become obstacles while you are trying to raise your children, such as laws, environment and outside distractions.

# CHAPTER 1
## VALUES, MORALS AND ETHICS

As a parent today you have inherited a very tough job in raising your children. This is a job I guarantee if done right will be the most rewarding thing you have ever undertaken in your life. On the other hand, it will be harder than any job you could take on to earn a living.

You have been tasked with protecting your child at all costs. It is your job to be a role model teaching them values, morals and ethics. These three simple words, as easy as they are to say, are not as easy to teach, and keep engraved in your child's mind.

The baby boomer generation were the last of the children who were raised with a mother figure at home. This parental figure managed the household while ensuring the children were taught the basic traits needed to be successful in society.

When the baby boomer generation grew up and became parents they started raising a new generation of kids who had no mother figure at home to teach them right from wrong. It was the breaking ground of what we now call latchkey kids.

Unfortunately another chain of events took place during this period of time; the removal of corporal punishment from the school systems throughout the nation, and the beginning of the removal of parents' rights to discipline their children.

In today's society the old traditional upbringing has been replaced by an economic driven upbringing, where there are no parents at home during the day to teach the children and guide them. In a lot of cases the child pretty much raised themselves.

Economics has dictated the average household will require both parents to work to survive in today's economy. With the lack of parental oversight, today's children are pretty much being raised by the likes of reality TV and video games.

In today's society it appears many parents have failed to achieve instilling values, morals and ethics in their children. It has been documented in many studies conducted in recent years, indicating young adults leaving home today lack a grasp of what is right or wrong and what it means to be responsible. These basic skills are very important to a child's success as an adult in society.

Children today lack the concept of being responsible for their own actions, as well as the actions of those who enter their environment. If someone close to them is in need, they fail to supply them with help, comfort, guidance and safety if necessary. For instance, one of the simplest things such as taking care of a loved one who is sick or looking in on an elderly family member, can be no simple task for them. A lot of young adults today just do not want to be bothered with such responsibility.

Due to a lack of values being taught at home, kids today have established their own set of values. These values are based on, "It's me against the world," "I will survive at all costs," "It's not fair," and the fact that they want to hold little to no responsibility as they move through life.

I truly believe we as parenting adults have allowed ourselves to be consumed by the rat race We have allowed economics to run our lives and take the place of grooming ours children to succeed in life. Yes, I fully understand it takes two working parents to survive today. As much of a shame as it is, it is very true.

As parents we must interact with our children, no matter how tired we are after a long day at work. It's our job to stimulate and lead their young minds to commit to values. Teaching them values is not enough. You must ensure they are applying them. You have to enforce values that will become a part of your child's identity.

It is important that your child acquires a healthy sense of guilt for doing wrong. They must understand a lie is a breach of trust, and is not acceptable within society. They must learn empathy to give them the ability to be caring toward others.

Talk to your children about values and provide examples when having a general conversation with them. Teach responsibility by having them do their chores. Yes, it is much faster to do it yourself, but the child does not learn anything when you do it for them. Then you have to ask yourself, am I willing to be their maid for the rest of my life?

While keeping within your child's maturity level, nurture his or her young mind with knowledge and skills. You must establish how much information their young minds can absorb at different age levels. They need to learn the importance of taking on responsibility, and how to manage criticism, to enable them to overcome the hurdles in life.

Your task as a parenting role model will not be easy. You must learn to be strong, caring and persistent while running into many obstacles. There will be times when you just want to give up, but know you cannot, because giving up means giving up on your child.

In the '50s and '60s, the average household only had one parent working, while the other parent took on the responsibility of taking care of the family and home. This in

itself is a full-time job. The parent at home becomes the major influence, the teacher of values, while monitoring their child's daily routine.

Today in most households there is no parent at home. The kids are pulled out of bed and whisked off to a daycare provider in the early morning. Daycare providers are in business to make money. Simple math tells them the more kids they have, the more money they make.

At some point they end up with more kids than they can safely watch, resulting in the kids babysitting each other, as well as teaching each other every bad habit in the book. Economics today has all but made an at-home parent extinct.

It takes two parents today to keep a household alive financially. Each aspect of life you come in contact with wants a piece of your paycheck.

Then you have states that make laws requiring you to pay outside entities for services provided, whether you want them or not, such as insurance companies. When such laws are put in place the end result is that the entities raise the price of what they want for the service rendered. They do this because you have no choice but to pay for it.

The mother figure used to stay home and nurture the minds of their children, while the father was expected to earn a living. Then in the late '60s and early '70s more and more women started to go to work. The Equal Rights Amendment for women was making strong headway.

Now let me go on record saying, I totally believe in ERA for women. I believe a woman in the work force should be treated and paid as well as any man. The reason I brought up ERA is that like many movements, it had a heavy influence on our young ladies becoming professional women and not a stay-at-home mom. Ultimately that had a negative impact on our children.

I believe more and more women entered the work force during this period of time  because of ERA. Two parents now working has resulted in the average family household income increasing.

Corporations, who produce products pay survey companies big money to find out, which products the public need and/or want to buy. They also tell them how much money they can charge for their products, based on the average household income of an area. Thus the costs of products keep going up each year.

All in all today's children are latchkey kids, with both parents having to work just to cloth and feed them. Values, morals and ethics were once a strong quality in our children as they made their way into society. Now the parent-teacher at home has been replaced by the teacher's aid and role models called reality TV and the entertainment industry and every violent video game you can think of.

Life in general has been filled with so many distractions and it seems the role of a parent has become very difficult. If both parents do not work then it means the family will do without. If both parents work, then they are both too tired after a full day's work to give their children 100% of their attention.

I have listened to a lot of the Great Depression generation talk about how they were very poor growing up. Back then if they wanted a toy, they made it. Stores back in the Depression years and before only carried what was needed for a household to survive and today the shelves are loaded with everything you can imagine.

The dust bowl generation of adults indicates that as kids they had nothing and they turned out just fine. Yes, that is true, they did turn out fine. The Great Depression children are probably the most responsible generation this country has ever produced in its history. They are good with money and they have very few needs.

But the big reason they turned out so well was everybody who surrounded them were also poor. There were very few who had money to waste, and a huge population of poor across the nation. The population of poor was so large the kids growing up did not think much about being poor.

In today's society there is a very distinct line between those who have money and those who do not. This is very evident to parents, causing them to strive hard to give their children what they can. Because of the pressures in life to keep up with those around you, it has impacted the quality time spent raising your children.

The teaching of values, morals and ethics starts with the child observing their parents in action. Your child growing up has a mind that is maturing on a daily basis, taking in everything mom and dad say and do.

In their minds if their parents do it or say it, it must be OK for them to follow suit. To show you how fast those minds mature and compute knowledge, I recently watched a three year old sitting and playing a video game on his parent's phone. He worked that phone like he was a wizard at it.

When young adults become parents, the things they say and do in front of their children which are deemed less than moral have to come to a stop. At this point in your life you made a choice to advance your bond with each other by bringing another human life into existence.

The days of partying and staying up to the early hours of the morning are over. Those days of sleeping in until noon are also gone. You as a parent have a responsibility to get up early and get your child's routine going.

Parents who sleep in leaving their child crib bound in a dark room until noon are being neglectful. This type of early upbringing for a toddler can lead to emotional problems down the road, such as lack of social skills, or bouts of anger.

This fragile being will look to you for protection, security, love, comfort, food and teachings. As their mind matures, you can see they are mimicking you every move you make or say. At this point they do not know right from wrong. The simplest thing, such as keeping up with another sibling, can be frustrating for them, because their mind and body have not learned to work together in unison.

Babies lay on the floor and even though their bodies are unable to move as of yet, their eyes follow you around the room. I believe an infant's mind matures faster than their motor skills, and the reason those eyes are following your motion is because they are learning, as well as searching for security.

Whether you realize it or not, you have become a role model from the time your child is born. You are their caregiver and they will see the world through you. The principles you set will be their principles. You need to be careful with your actions displayed in front of your young child. They will assume your action, such as hitting someone, is OK, thus they will mimic it by hitting other children.

Your profanity has to come to a stop, because the first word out of their mouth won't be mommy or daddy, it will be an unkind word. When adults utilize profanity they seem to emphasize it in their speech, making it stand out over all other words used. This outburst of emotion will catch the infant's attention quickly, resulting in you living through many embarrassing moments when you least expect it.

A big task ahead of you as your child develops will be to teach them values, morals and ethics. The saying "Live by example" definitely applies here. You cannot expect your child to learn these traits if you do not portray them in front of them. The saying "Do as I say and not as I do" does not work out well in the end.

It is important for you to become a pertinent part of your child's life. You have to teach your child values. They must have something they believe in lasting  beliefs or ideals that cannot be influenced by a negative environment. A set of standards in which good or bad and desirable or undesirable are distinguished.

Allow your children to be children. Do not make them grow up too fast, but allow them to be innocent as long as they can. Keep their fantasy world alive, such as Santa Clause, the Tooth Fairy and the Easter Bunny. It teaches them to have something to believe in, and it gives them something to look forward to. It will also teach them to respect their parents for all they went through to keep their innocent fantasies alive.

Make the holidays as special as you can for your children. Their memories of the holidays at home will be their fondest memories, which they will harbor for the rest of their lives. The traditions you teach them will be continued when they raise their children.

The family values you instill in your child will influence their behavior and attitude, having an impact on them establishing guidelines in regards to how they will respond in any situation that confronts them. Values can come in the form of religious beliefs, such as do unto others as you would have them do unto you. They also come in the form of right from wrong.

You need to spend a lot of time during the course of raising your child teaching them right from wrong, sensitivity and compassion. A child who is raised by a sensitive person develops a sense of being well balanced, has a good sense of well-being, and will be able to share that sensitivity with others.

At some point they will leave the secure nest of home for short periods of time each day. They will find themselves surrounded by every aspect of good and bad the world has to offer. The time you put into preparing them for this day will pay off for them as well as for you down the road.

Your child will be faced with many trials in life when you are not around. How they react to these trials will determine how well you got your message across to them. A very common value test, which occurs amongst children these days, happens when they come in contact with a less fortunate child who does not fit into their social structure.

It may be a child that everyone knows to be poor and wears torn or worn out clothes to school every day. The alpha child (leader) of the social group decides it would be funny to go over and tease this child who is less fortunate, who a lot of times is ostracized from all groups.

The test will be how will your child reacts to this. Will they fall back on their learned values, putting a stop to it before it occurs, or will they push their learned values aside to please their friends? An even more important question for you as a parent is how you will react if your child crosses the line, disregarding the values you have instilled in them, just to please their friends.

We all want to believe all we have to do is tell our children the difference between right and wrong and the lesson is learned. Not true. You will have to re-enforce right from wrong many times over with different scenarios. Most children will try you, which will result in another lesson being learned, namely the consequences for doing wrong.

How about morals? The definition of morals is, "A lesson, especially one concerning what is right or prudent, that can be derived from a story, a piece of information, or an experience. A person's standards of behavior or beliefs concerning what is and is not acceptable for them to do."

Let's talk about the different types of morals and how they apply to our children in society. A moral attitude is the manner in which you have taught your child to conduct themselves while in the company of others or the principles which they base a decision on, which may have a direct impact on others. The basis to distinguish right from wrong comes from their mindset and attitude.

A moral person establishes a positive attitude and a set of guidelines by which they will differentiate between what is considered right conduct and wrong conduct. They will do everything in their power to be honest, leading the way by example while being an upright pillar in the community. They will oppose immoral actions by others.

It is important that your child knows they must tell the truth at all times. They must convey the truth to others when interacting within their social group. It is important they understand that standing up for what is right is not necessarily going to make them the most popular person amongst their peers.

While raising your child you will need to instill in them what is called a moral obligation. This is a responsibility to always do the right thing when making decisions. The obligation to inform an adult of a wrong which has occurred. This is where it is very important you have a close bond with your child; a bond that makes them feel like they can tell you anything.

The foundation of your child's moral lessons are formed on what you call the moral being. It allows them to be able to recognize, decipher and conform to all the rules of what is right, which you, the parent, and society have established for them to follow.

Moral support is taught at home on a daily basis by you, the parent. It is shown in the manner you support your child's decision making and endeavors in life. It is a support factor where you encourage your child to not be afraid to challenge themselves. It gives your child the confidence that you will be there for them at all times. This is a trait of trust, and when learned, they will show their support for others as well.

You should strive to go with them to every function they are involved in. The day will come soon enough when they will want their own space, not needing you with them wherever they go. Even though life is very busy, you need to set aside the time to be at every event they participate in, football, ballet, cheerleading, basketball etc. Just you making the effort to be there makes them feel like a winner, even if they do not get into the game.

Over years of coaching football, I have seen so many sad faces on children. They look to the stands just to catch a glimpse of their parents, who told them they would be there. The look on their faces told me without words, the parents did not show up.

I have seen young adults on senior night in high school having to be walked onto the football field by other kids' parents or coaches, because their parents did not care enough to be there for them.

Remember this saying, the time you put into your kids is what you will get out of them in return. If you cannot be there for them growing up, they will not be there for you when you grow old and frail.

It is important that your child fully understands your rules of morals and conduct which you expect them to conduct themselves by. This leads to your child being sound in decision making, with the confidence to determine right from wrong.

Ethics is simple motivation to do right rather than wrong. In today's work environment there are a lot of people lacking ethics. You come across people who cut corners while doing their job. They cut corners because it gets their job done faster, but it does not necessarily produce the right outcome for another person.

It might be a person who makes decisions that impact other peoples' lives, and instead of approaching the decision making process in a impartial manner, they take only their own personal opinion or beliefs into consideration to render their decision.

Ethics are rules which are explicitly adopted by a group of people. It is rules or standards governing the conduct of a person or the members of a group. It is the intent to render a decision or act in a manner with sound principles.

Ethics dictates that you understand there will be consequences for improper decision making, and challenges you to make sound moral decisions. Your child must understand if they fail to do so, they will be judged by those surrounding them.

You need to teach them by portraying good ethics, while making the right decisions. You need make them understand doing the right thing will not always make them the most popular person with their peers. They're going to be surrounded by kids who do not have good ethics. Kids who base their decision making on what is best for them and do not care how it impacts other people.

# CHAPTER 2
## RESPONSIBILITY/ACCOUNTABILITY

Like values, morals and ethics, responsibility and accountability are such important traits young adults must possess to be successful in today's world. The simplest thing as showing responsibility establishes trust with other people.

When was the last time you saw an employer hire someone who had a track record of not being dependable? Getting a job today is based partially on a person showing they are responsible and are dependable. If the employer cannot trust you, then you will not be around very long.

A child is not born with the responsibility trait, it is a learned trait which is supposed to be taught to them by their parents verbally and through actions. It is a trait that can be started at an early age, such as a toddler being taught to assist a parent figure in cleaning up their toys.

Parents can make a game out of these learning sessions to keep the toddler's attention. Establish rules for them to follow and if they stay within your established guidelines by keeping their mess located where it is supposed to be, then you have taught your child a responsibility trait.

Responsibility and accountability come in many forms, such as chores at home, schoolwork, charity work, working to make extra money and taking care of other people's needs. Accountability is simple. A child is taught to be a person of their word. If they tell grandma they will mow the lawn, then they need to do exactly that, no matter what comes up.

It is important that you show affection by praising them when they accomplish a goal you have set for them. There is nothing worse than trying your hardest to please someone and getting no acknowledgment in return. When you make a big deal out of something they accomplish no matter how little it was, their eyes light up like it is the best thing that has ever happened to them.

While working in the prison, if an inmate did something worth being praised for, I gave them the praise they had coming, and like a child their eyes would light up, making them try twice as hard the next time. A lot of these guys in prison never received praise or affection as a child. That is part of the reason why they ended up where there at. Do not make this mistake with your children. Do not be afraid to show affection.

A child learns a lot of their lessons in life by observing those who are constantly around them. With this being said, it is very important, for you as a parent to teach your kids to be responsible by acting as a responsible adult. They watch you closely. They hear more of your conversations with another adult than you think.

Example: Your mother-in-law called you asking you to come over and mow her lawn on the only day off you have had in two weeks. During the conversation you told her you would come by the next day and mow it. The next morning you get up and decide you would rather go fishing. It is your only day off and you have worked hard to get this little bit of pleasure. So you tell your wife you are going to call her mom and tell her you feel sick today and will mow her lawn next week after work.

Meanwhile your child overhears the conversation. Your child just learned two lessons in life. The first lesson is it is OK to lie, and the second lesson is it is OK not to be responsible and keep your word.

It is your job as a parent to assign your child responsibilities they can reasonably accomplish; such as taking out the garbage, and taking care of their pets.

I see 99% of the children beg and turn on the waterworks to get a pet. The first couple days they are inseparable, then the newness of it wears off and guess who gets to clean up after them and feeding them? Yes, you.

Look, we are all guilty of this, including me, but most of the time when a child wants a pet, I usually hear their parents clearly tell them before they say yes, it will be their responsibility to feed and clean up after them. But it seems in most cases we do not follow through, and you see the parent outside cleaning up after the animal.

Try this the next time your child wants something. Make up a contract with them and have them sign it. That way you have something physical to refer back to when they start stumbling.

A contract can be used for just about anything. Let's say your child wants their first car, but you have stipulations for them obtaining it to be accompanied by penalties for not holding up their end of the deal.

Put it in a written contract between you and them, make them read it and sign it, then frame it and hang it where they can see it every day as a reminder. It is all about accountability and re-sponsibility.

They must understand their word is their bond in life. All of this is being said because stud-ies have shown children are leaving home with a lack of morals and values. Parent have gotten so involved with waiting on their children hand and foot that they are losing necessary basic traits such as responsibility. Young adults today are showing a strong trait of being irresponsible.

When a child is missing basic traits, such as responsibility and accountability, they do not feel the need to nurture other people, but rather they only feel the need to just take care of themselves. Studies are also indicating the lack of this trait leads to taking shortcuts in life such as cheating in school, and in some cases taking things that do not belong to them.

Crime amongst teenagers has escalated with those children who possess a lack of responsibili-ty and accountability. A lot of these young adults refuse to take responsibility for their negative actions, thus blaming everyone except for them-selves for their bad behavior. The prison system is loaded with these types of people.

The lack of possessing the responsibility trait makes them feel they have been victimized by so-ciety, after being judged by their peers. They feel people surrounding them need to just mind their own business and allow them to do as they wish. They do not feel anybody should hold them accountable nor responsible for their actions.

These criminals are not unlike a little child who has been caught doing something wrong. If you ask them if they committed the crime they are in prison for, they will tell you they were framed. They will make up many excuses to keep from exposing themselves as being guilty.

It is your role as a parent to instill responsibility and accountability into your child. They need to learn it is very important to make choices which are considered responsible, and follow through with them. They also need to understand we all make mistakes, but it is important to accept guilt and be honest when they are confronted about it. It is their obligation to possess qualities such as fairness, respect, courage, honesty, compassion and accountability.

They must be taught to act on their values and morals, while standing up for principles they believe in. We must take the time to insure our children have self respect, and respect for us, the parent, as well as others.

Teaching your child responsibility does not take place while you are cleaning up after the mistakes they make in life. They must be held accountable when they fail to follow through with a responsibility you have assigned them, such as cleaning their room, picking up after themselves and not leaving it for mother the maid. You should also not be guilty of doing their homework for them. It is also not good for you to jump off the couch to make them a snack just because they say they're hungry.

You must not become an enabler for your children. When they hit a certain age they are fully capable of fixing a sandwich for themselves. If you do not teach them to be responsible enough to get up and eat on their own, you will wake up one day with a 25-year-old adult sprawled out on your couch. They will be barking out orders to their parents to make them a sandwich. You have to remind them from time to time, you are not their servant, nor their maid.

Responsibility is a taught trait, which means you must lead them by the hand and teach them how to perform the task at hand to your satisfaction. If they do not know what your guidelines are, then they will make their own, and it probably will not be up to your standards. As a child, by taking care of their assigned responsibilities they are showing you respect.

What about the times when your child is around other people and they tell you what a delight he or she is to be around? Yet at home getting them to do chores is like pulling teeth. They have with those people what you must get established at home in your own relationship with your child. That is respect and a certain amount of fear for failing to be responsible.

They're such a pleasure around other people because they do not know how a person outside the family will hold them accountable or react to wrongdoing. It comes down to uncertainty, the fear of the unknown.

Responsibility has to be taught. If it is not, there will be hard lessons to be learned along the way in life. When it come s to the work force, getting hired depends on a responsible work history.

Keeping a job is based on that person being responsible enough to show up for work on time, as well as being accountable and productive.

Responsibility comes in so many forms. One very important form is taking responsibility for one's actions. A lot of criminals have trouble in this area. They cannot seem to take full responsibility for their actions. They prey on the weak instead of helping them. They know right from wrong, but they still commit the crimes.

It is imperative you hold your kids accountable for breaking household rules. If you do not, your child may venture out and break the rules society as put in place. When criminals break the law, it gets a little easier each time.

# CHAPTER 3
## ESTABLISH GOALS

Goal setting can open up the world to a young child, yet it is heavily overlooked by parents, whether it is short term goals or long term goals. A short term goal is something you can achieve in a day or week, such as fixing your grades or eating better.

Long term goals take a year or more to accomplish, such as saving money to buy a car, or getting very good grades in academic courses you need to get accepted into an elite university. But nevertheless teenagers are young and vibrant, and goals are the means by which a person will reach success in life. It is an obstacle or group of obstacles one must focus on conquering to achieve a certain goal in life.

Teenagers are not born knowing how to establish goals, this is something that has to be taught to them. In the eyes of a teenager, choosing a life-changing goal can be a lot to handle, especially since today's society has an endless supply of goals that one can choose from.

While my son was growing up, all he could talk about was being a professional football player. Even though this was a goal considered by most to be impossible to achieve, I supported him from the first time he brought it up. I started off by explaining to him how hard it was to become a professional athlete. I then explained to him professional athletes were not born that way, but rather became exceptional athletes from a lot of sacrifice and hard work.

I was always up front with him about the likelihood of him actually getting into professional football. I told him I would train him to take a run at becoming a professional football player, if he was willing to sacrifice and work hard. Now mind you this started at age nine. Not only did I work with his athletic ability and sharpen his motor skills, but I also felt the mental part of the training was very important, such as achieving milestones that I established for him along the way.

We established one goal at a time, and once the goal was achieved, we moved on to the next established goal. I vividly remember his very first goal was to get his leg strong enough to kick a Point After Touchdown (PAT). Once he achieved that milestone his next goal was to be the first kid in our area playing Pop Warner and to kick a 35-yard field goal during a game. He achieved that goal.

The next reachable goal was for him to be recognized by the local high school coaches as a "must have" player. He achieved this goal as well. Then we established a goal for him to make the newspaper after each high school game to get exposure. The next goal was to get recognized by colleges across the nation. He established that goal and went on to play college football in Wisconsin.

The final goal was to get his shot at professional football. He accomplished this goal by getting invited to a professional kicking combine. Now did he get into professional football? No, but he learned so much along the way about responsibility and accountability, and he learned he had to work hard to achieve goals in life.

The lessons of life he learned along the way were priceless; lessons such as hard work pays off, learning how to cope with failure, being turned down, coping with injuries and still being able to perform. These were all priceless lessons in life. My point is that he was always so busy accomplishing goals that he never gave us any trouble during his teenage years.

As you noticed these were all simple goals established in a proper order. Remember, never deflate a child's ambitions, no matter how ridiculous it seems to you, or how far- fetched they seem to be. You must be there and support them all the way. It is OK to let them know that some goals are very hard to reach, but as long as they are willing to try, then you will be in their corner all the way.

Now as a parent I want you to know that when a child sets a goal which is a very high mark, such as being a professional athlete, that child will have to sacrifice. When other kids are watching cartoons they will be outside practicing. In conjunction with this you as a parent will also sacrifice your time to be there to assist them and in most cases supply money to assist them in reaching their goal.

But goal setting in life is a must. It is the road to success. It establishes a sense of direction for the child to go. If your child wants to become a doctor their goals will look like this.

1. To have excellent grades throughout school.
2. Take every college prep class available.
3. Get accepted to a university.
4. Get accepted into medical school
5. Graduate. This is what it takes to achieve success.

There is nothing I hate worse than talking to a child who has no clue what they are going to do after high school. This means their parents failed to establish or even talk to them about goals. This shows me there is a lack of a bond between child and parents.

Goals are the driving force by which we function in life. A lot of people do not realize they set goals every day, such as creating a want list—motorcycles , cars and vacations. Whether or not they achieve these goals is based on how hard they work toward their goal at hand.

By having established goals in place, it makes a child's life more organized and in order. Talk to your child. Ask them what they want to be when they grow up, and start laying out achievable goals for them to reach. This will reinforce the fact that you are there to support them, and you will see them blossom in front of your eyes. Goals are very important in structuring a young person's life.

As a parent it is very important for you to enforce the fact that if you do not succeed at first with a particular goal, then try, try again. Do not let your child give up on themselves, because any phase of their goals is too hard. Be there to support them, while helping them get over the hurdle. They will thank you later, and also you do not want them to receive the message it is OK to just quit when things get a little hard. Being a quitter becomes an easy solution to any adverse situation they may face.

After all it is their goals they set for themselves to reach. They need to learn responsibility and push through the rough times they will face. Goal setting is the road to success.

# CHAPTER 4
## SPORTS INTERACTION

Youth sports is a very controversial issue amongst psychiatrists and some medical doctors. It is controversial because there are so many adults coaching youth sports today who have no business coaching. Simply put, a lot of them possess bad values and morals.

Psychiatrists believe there are too many coaches emphasizing winning at all costs over the more positive things that can come out of playing sports, such as social interaction, learning to be competitive amongst their peers and learning to win and lose with grace. They believe this type of adult influence can lead to bad morals and values being passed on to your child.

After years of coaching sports and being involved from Pop Warner to college levels, as well as sitting on two boards as a vice president governing youth football, I have to agree that there are many coaches who do not belong on the field interacting with our kids. A lot of the time adults forget why they are teaching a child about sports. Too many times coaches allow their inner competitiveness and the importance of winning at all costs to take over the good things they could be teaching children as they play sports.

During my five years on the youth football board, we did our best to weed out bad coaches. We conducted background checks on all applicants for criminal history. But unfortunately there is no background check for ethics and morals. Over the years we fired a lot of coaches, but it was not until their bad side surfaced. On the flip side, I have come across less than ethical board members in various communities who will support coaches who displayed bad morals and values.

In small towns, high schools have big traditions. These traditions are passed on to the kids attending those schools and stand out when they become adult alumni. It is not unusual to come across administrators who promote a "win at all costs" attitude to their alumni and students for the sake of the school's name. I say this because I have seen this ugly snake rear its head on more than one occasion.

For example, I remember once there was a coach in the local newspaper facing termination as an educator and coach at a local high school. According to the article, this individual allowed students on his team to watch porn while at school, which he had supplied. Now this is a clear example of very bad morals, values and ethics.

Let's look at the impact "win at all costs" can have on generations of kids going through a school system which breeds this type of attitude, and how it affects kids as they become adults. We will look at one of several responses which were written in the newspaper by alumni after they read the article about their favorite coach being suspended pending investigation. There were actually alumni members of this high school who wrote in supporting the coach.

They indicated that although the coach was wrong for showing his players porn, his dismissal may be going overboard and would leave a huge void in the athletic program. If this coach was let go their winning tradition may have taken a set-back. This is the type of people and attitude we are trying to keep away from our children.

Medical doctors see numerous sports related injuries every year. Most of these injuries are re-lated to over-training fatigued muscles. The big trend today is club sports or what they call travel-ing teams, which goes almost year around. These teams are made up of the best local talent, and promote a higher level of competition to promote your child's ability to colleges.

In most cases these types of teams put a tre-mendous amount of pressure on a young child to perform to their highest potential. Children who participate on these teams hit burnout quickly. They are not allowed to have a life, because their current life is consumed with practice and going out of town each weekend to play in scheduled games.

Needless to say, if you have a child playing on such a team, you the parent no longer have a life either. The cost to participate in this sport will also put a strain on your bank account due to traveling from town to town and sometimes spending the night.

As a coach I was never fond of traveling teams. In my eyes a child should be playing a sport to have fun and secondly to further their ability to achieve future goals by utilizing their athletic talent. I have often heard parents complaining about the cost and the burden these traveling teams place on them, and for the life of me I cannot understand why parents put their kids through this.

When a kid is ten they do not need pressure to perform with perfection. Skills come from practicing. Their skills get better with practice and competing year in year out. When you place your child on a traveling team they usually have tough rules to abide by, which means fun is out the door.

Just stick with city sports and high school sports. The process of getting your child noticed by recruiters comes from promotion of their talent via video. I will not go too far into this, but as a prior recruiter for a university, the promotion aspect has to come from the child with an active role from their parents. Do not expect the local high school coach to promote your child with the recruiters. Most of them take on the attitude when the season is over, it is time to relax and de-stress, thus no promoting is taking place.

Sport in itself is so important in a child's life. It teaches them interaction skills with other people and they will make a lot of friends along the way. It helps them understand they have to work in conjunction with other people to achieve a specific goal. These are all skills that will be needed as an adult when they enter the work force.

Employers today ask a lot of question about teamwork during interviews. If you are a person who never played a sport, then you will have a hard time achieving teamwork type goals.

Sport is a perfect tool to teach children about life's experiences, such as losing and not always being first. Life is full of pitfalls. A person is not always going to be first or the best. The lessons learned from sports will teach young adults that they will not always achieve a specific goal on the first go round, such as applying for a promotion. What sport does teach a child is that if you get knocked down get up, brush yourself off and try again.

These are definitely life lessons to be learned. Learning these lessons early in life makes it easier to accept rejection in a manner that is conducive to trying harder the next time.

Now what type of coach do you want grooming your child's young mind? The type you are looking for is a person that is an outstanding role model. This person must not have values that indicate they want to win at all costs. I am sorry to tell you this, but after being a coach on a football field for 12 years and a college recruiter for two years, I know you are going to run into this personality.

This is the type of coach you do not want around your child. Win at all costs usually means cheating and this is one of the traits we are trying to keep out of our kids. The other negative influence is the parent-coach who starts his kid over everybody else no matter how bad they are. They go into every game just praying their kid will get better and not stand out like a sore thumb.

When you first introduce your young child to sports, the coaches are going to be people who have kids on the team. That's the reason they are coaching. The younger the age group of children, the less seasoned the coach is going to be. Be helpful with these guys, even though they may have some knowledge of the game. They are still trying to figure out the coaching aspect of the sport.

You hope you will get a coach who is a very mild-mannered person when your kid is first starting out. One bad experience can end a child's will to play sports ever again. All in all there are a lot of good coaches out there. If you come across one who is a little rough around the collar then let him know to back off a little. Sometimes that is all it takes to make them take a look at themselves in the mirror.

My wife and I raised three children. I never gave them a choice whether or not they wanted to play sports. I always signed them up while making a deal with them; if they did not like the sport they were signed up for, then after the season was over they did not have to play it again.

The reason I said I never gave them a choice is children are always afraid to try new things, and getting them out of their comfort zone sometimes has to be pushed on them. They are naturally hesitant to intermingle with new kids. So the moral of the story is, if you ask them if they would like to sign up for a sport, they will more than likely say no.

I will forewarn you about upper level sports, such as high school and college. These coaches' jobs depend on winning games. Most of the coaches I have met over the years are very good with teens. They all have a rough quality about them because they must command respect from their players, but many of them would give the shirt off their back if one of their players were in need.

Yes, in the upper levels of sports you will see a win at all cost attitude. Little things such as playing students who do not have a qualifying GPA sometimes happen. Sooner or later you read about this type of coach being caught and fired. The program they represented usually will end up with sanctions placed against them. College sports are in the paper all the time for recruiting violations and playing players who are academically ineligible. These are generally not bad coaches, but coaches driven to stretch the rules to keep their jobs.

With all I just said that was discouraging, I want you to understand sport is a tool to teach your children about life experiences. If you as a parent get yourself caught up in thinking your child should be starting over other kids, this is a battle you will lose every time. We all want to believe our child is better than other children at everything they do. It is a natural instinct. But take a step back and remember your child is there to have fun and learn lessons while perfecting their skills in the sport they like.

When you get to the upper level sports there are a lot of factors playing into a coach deciding who starts and who rides the pine. And remember, high school sports are not like Pop Warner. Every player does not have to be played. The coaches at this level are playing their best players in an effort to win.

Although I just dampened your mood about sports, they bring a lot of good qualities to the table. Your child will get plenty of exercise and develop physical skills. They will learn about fair play and how to interact with others. Fun will automatically come to the forefront along with self esteem.

While playing sports they should learn to have a good attitude, which will follow them into adulthood. Make sure the environment is a learning atmosphere, teaching positive values and behavior traits.

If you are having a coach related issue, talk to the coach alone away from the kids. Find a common ground or direction the kids should be going in. If that does not work then you will have to go up the chain of command.

Another good quality about sports is that they keep idle minds occupied. What this means is your child is least likely to go out and get into trouble if they are playing a sports. Surveys conducted indicate 92% of female athletes are less likely to take drugs and 80% less likely to become pregnant. Boys are less likely to go out and get into trouble, because their leisure time is preoccupied with scheduled activities.

# CHAPTER 5
## CORPORAL PUNISHMENT

This chapter was written to express my concerns about the large number of our teenage population that has gotten out of control, while wreaking havoc in society. I feel this is in part due to corporal punishment laws being removed by most states and/or watered down. Prior to the 1980s, if parents and the school system felt it was necessary to spank a child for getting out of line, they did so with no questions asked.

After many years those against corporal punishment indicated it led to many emotional problems in children and also to child abuse. Corporal punishment has been gone for well over 25 years now in most states, and child abuse still firmly exists across the nation.

By the late 1980s most states had abolished corporal punishment leaving parents and the school system with very few avenues to discipline a child, other than written or verbal warnings. Parents for the most part have completely dropped the concept of spanking a child in today's society.

I want to go on record as saying I was never very fond of spanking my children, but if a situation came up and they needed it, then they got a spanking. My kids will be the first to tell you they did not receive many spankings and to be honest with you, it hurt me more to spank them than it hurt them.

Spanking was once a tool used to deter bad behavior, at home as well as in the school system. The child knew that getting spanked for bad behavior was a repercussion for the act they committed. In the school system children use to fear getting spanked for bad behavior. Now they fear nothing.

Advocates of school corporal punishment argue it provided an immediate response to bad behavior, resulting in the student quickly going back to the classroom where he or she could learn something. It was used in place of suspending a child from school. Opponents believe that other disciplinary methods are equally or more effective. Some regard it as tantamount to violence or abuse.

Opponents argue corporal punishment is linked to adverse physical, psychological and educational outcomes including, "increased aggressive and destructive behavior, increased disruptive classroom behavior, vandalism, poor school achievement, poor attention span, increased drop-out rate, school avoidance and school phobia, low self-esteem, anxiety, somatic complaints, depression, suicide and retaliation against teachers.

Now let's take a look at what the corporal punishment opponents argued above, and apply the current statistics released in 2012 by the Federal Bureau of Investigation, approximately 20 years after most states eliminated corporal punishment from their disciplinary process. Corporal

Punishment Opponents argued it caused the following:

**Increased aggressive and destructive behavior**-
Let's see. This behavior has not gotten any better. It is actually worst today. The FBI statistics report that amongst teens aggravated assaults as well as drug/narcotic and weapon violations have been on the rise since 2004.

Bullying remains one of the largest problems in schools, with the percentage of students reportedly bullied at least once per week steadily increasing since 1999. The number of girls involved in school crime has increased from over 12,000 incidents in 2000 to approximately 25,000 occurrences in 2005.

This included crimes ranging from those against property and society (criminal mischief, burglary, and drug/narcotic violations) to offenses against persons (assault, manslaughter and murder).

**School vandalism**- School vandalism has been on the rise nationally amongst approximately 89,000 public schools. Schools nationally report annually approximately 98,000 incidents. This counts only the incidents reported to insurance companies. Schools in California have virtually surrounded their campuses with chain link fencing, including padlocks for after hours. This is because vandalism has become uncontrollable. Classrooms are being broken into and destroyed, football fields torn to shreds by teens spinning circles on them with their vehicles.

Also graffiti has been a major issue, with gangs spraying their logos, and kids putting their moniker or nickname on school property. The next time a train goes through your town try to count how many cars have been vandalized.

**Poor school achievement**- Well, we do not have to go into this very deep. It is no secret that school testing results across the nation has been considered very poor for several years.

**School dropout rate**- The dropout rate in 1990 was 12% across the nation, and it has since dropped to 7%. The school attendance rates have been on the rise due to schools enforcing the truancy laws. Why are they enforcing them so hard now? Unlike in past years, schools now do not get paid for the days students miss school. It all comes down to economics. If the schools want to get paid, they have to enforce the truancy laws to ensure the students attend school.

**Low Self esteem**- This category seems to be still on the rise. Eating disorders in teens are a good indicator of self esteem related issues. The United States has become the role model for obesity and every fictitious diet plan some person can think up.

Statistics show 44% of teen girls and 15 % of teen boys are attempting to lose weight. Seventy % of girls age 15 to 17 avoid normal daily activities, such as attending school, when they feel bad about their looks. Nearly 40% of boys in middle school and high school regularly exercise with the goal of increasing muscle mass. About 20% of all teens will experience depression before they reach adulthood.

Leading psychiatrist and corporal punishment opponents felt corporal punishment was the cause of children's bad behavior traits at home and in the school system. Now 20 years later, after the removal of corporal punishment, bad behavior traits still exist and have worsened. This leaves some teachers and even parents in fear for their own safety.

If you look at the statistics regarding school related incidents, in combination with what we read every day in the newspapers about teens being in trouble, the removal of corporal punishment has created real problems in the school systems across the nation.

When corporal punishment was in place, it did in fact deter a large amount of teens from misbehaving. I wonder where the corporal punishment opponents are now, since the statistics show their theory was wrong.

This is why I strongly advise all parents to get involve with the politics that will affect them and their family down the road. Leading experts trying to make a name for themselves push their theories and ideals to politicians all the time. They think they have the miracle cure for all the ills of the world. But they do not publicize the negative aspect of their theory, and I wonder if some of them even look at the negative side.

For instance, medication, is intended to suppress or cure an ailment, but when you read the handout that you get with it, you will see it has 10 to 20 side effects that causes serious damage to other parts of your body. With any theory, there is a positive and negative side.

Look at California in 1993. The three strikes law was drafted to put serious violent criminals behinds bars for life. The legislators quickly drafted a bill and had people vote on it, and it passed overwhelmingly. But unfortunately they put the bill together so quickly that no one took into consideration all the gray areas in it, and how the District Attorneys across the state would take advantage of those loopholes by putting every criminal away under the three strikes law, including non-violent offenders.

After 20 years the prisons were two times over their legal capacity, resulting in the Federal Courts ordering the release of non-violent offenders, and the overhaul of the three strikes law.

All non-violent three strike cases were ordered to be reviewed for re-sentencing. Now what a waste of millions of tax payers' dollars. The reason I am mentioning this is people tend to create laws and push them hard because the time is right, but they usually fail to look at the future projected negative impact.

Corporal punishment in the schools started gradually going away in the 1980s and early 1990s. It had bad timing because prior to that the baby boomer generation was the first to raise children with both parents working.

Some people will say you still have the right to administer a spanking to a child if needed. What they fail to tell you is that if you leave a bruise on them it may be considered child abuse.

The removal of corporal punishment has left the schools with children who do not respect authority figures nor do some of them have respect for their own parents. The lack of corporal punishment in place at home and in the school system has left society with some of the most violent teenagers this country has ever seen. Due to the violence these teens are portraying, most states have taken up the practice of trying juveniles as adults for crimes.

Over the years interviewing young adults who took up a life of crime, they never told me once they became criminals because they received a spanking at home. Instead most of them pinpointed their failures in society to a lack of a proper upbringing; parents who did not care enough to correct them when they had done something wrong.

During the late 1960s and early 1970s, I remember hearing adults talking about Dr. Spock and his theories about raising children. At the time I never really paid much attention to what was being said. I had no clue what kind of impact Dr. Spock's theories would have on the lives of future adults and children.

Like most documented theorists, they themselves cannot predict the direct impact their theories will have on society. The impact usually comes many years down the road, at the hands of people who take a person's documented work and go overboard with it.

Humans are creatures of habit who are always looking for something to believe in. When they find a theory they like, they have a habit of adding to it, by incorporating their own beliefs and ideas. In this case it was the baby boomer generation, who were the young adults in the 1960s when Dr. Spock's book *Baby and Child Care* made a resurgence.

Dr. Benjamin McLane Spock, who was a brilliant pediatrician, originally wrote his book in 1946. This book had many great impacts on our medical society in regard to how babies should be handled during the infant stage. Dr. Spock himself was very advanced for his time period. He was a brilliant man who set marks for the medical society to follow.

Dr. Spock also had his political views and was a very liberal minded individual who was involved with the Socialist Workers Party in 1968. He wrote a book entitled *Dr. Spock on Vietnam.* Spock being a member of the left activist group was very outspoken against our troops and their mission in Vietnam.

Although I believe we had no business in Vietnam, due to it being nothing more than a Central Intelligence Agency power play, I do firmly believe we must support our troops. Remember these young men were not given a vote on whether they wanted to be there or not. They were drafted.

In Dr. Spock's writings he enforced the need for parents to be more flexible and affectionate with their children, and to treat them as individuals. I agree with all of this. A parent must be flexible during certain development stages of a child's early life, especially while they are learning right from wrong. And it is always important for a parent to show love, affection and passion toward their children, because it is a learned trait, and it reassures them of their environment.

But unfortunately in today's society, I feel a lot of kids have parents so consumed by everyday life, they fail their mission as parents. They raise their kids with a lack of shown affection and little to no quality time spent with them. In the end the child is an individual left raising themselves, setting their own standards on how life should and should not be.

The other day I came across a young lady with a tattoo on her shoulder that said "me against the world." Her body language was harsh and I instantly felt she was one of those children who received very little love or affection and raised herself.

Dr. Spock's books were also credited in the late 1960s with having a very large impact on the younger "hippie" generation. His literature influenced many young people to join rebellious groups and become activists against those fighting in Vietnam. It has been said Dr. Spock denied any claims that his book influenced young adults to take on his opinion about the war.

The 1960s was a volatile era, with a young generation struggling to find itself in the midst of experimenting with drugs, and rebelling against a traditional family upbringing. From that generation came extremists who took Dr. Spock's theories on child rearing, and combined them with their own beliefs.

Dr. Spock's books definitely had an impact on the young generation during that era; an impact that we are still feeling today. It molded a generation of people to be more liberal minded. As these young people went on to college, they became adults holding influential positions, thus influencing future laws such as those regarding corporal punishment. Dr. Spock's opinions then started impacting the nation and its laws by which it was run.

One of the impacts we have felt is the gradual elimination of all corporal punishment laws throughout the nation, state by state. The main law I am talking about is the ability for parents and the schools to spank a child for misbehaving.

Sure the laws say you can still discipline your child, but heaven forbid if you do it in public or leave a mark on their little behind. In most states if you leave a bruise or a mark on a child it will be considered excessive punishment, landing you in jail for child abuse.

Our children have lost grasp of all morals, which were suppose to be taught at home, by their parents. Respect for the role model type person no longer exists. Teachers no longer have control over their classrooms because they have no recourse to deal with bad behavior, other than sending the student to the principal's office. The same principal who has a long line of kids coming to his office for the same thing every day. Eventually the principal gets tired of dealing with these kids, who are being sent to him for intimidating their teachers and causing disruption in the classroom.

In the end, all he does is make them sit in his office until the next period starts and sends them on their way, to wreak havoc with the next teacher. Meanwhile the child is not receiving a proper education because they have learned all it takes to get out of class is to create a disturbance.

These are young minds. If their parents have not helped them establish goals in their life, then they do not know what they want out of life. Kids do not start to understand what direction their life is heading, until they get into their early twenties. The only thing they do know while they attend school is that they are bored with American History and they hate math, because they just do not understand it.

When I was growing up corporal punishment was still in place, and if you crossed the line with a teacher you met a wood paddle in the hallway. If you refused to accept the punishment then you were suspended for three days and sent home to your parents.

Believe me, when you met the paddle in the hallway, you were more than happy to sit in your seat and act right. And if you were suspended then you got to look forward to dealing with your parents at home, which may not have been as kind as being paddled.

The wood paddle laying on the teacher's desk hardly ever found use other than collecting dust. Its main job throughout the school year was to be a deterrent. There was not a day that went by you did not see that paddle, and it was always in the students' minds. I think part of the reason the wood paddle was so effective as a deterrent was the embarrassment it caused.

The thought that all your peers knew you just got your butt busted for being a fool was a future deterrent, for you and all other students. I know that those entwined in psychiatric theories, believe you should never embarrass a child. But we all know there are times when our children have to learn those little embarrassing lessons in life. Many famous authors have written over the years that there is a time when we must be humbled.

I remember a time when I was a young boy, and my mom told me it was time for dinner. I was sitting on the floor doing something and I told her I would be there in a minute. I must have used a rough tone of voice, because it was just a matter of seconds before my stepfather had me snatched up and told me I would get to the table now.

I still remember that to this day, lesson learned. Be careful how you speak to other people when you are preoccupied. Now when my wife says, "Honey, dinner is ready," I wrap up what I am doing and go to the dinner table. It's a lesson of respect.

Now I do not remember too many times as a child receiving a spanking, because it did not take many to get my attention. And I do not remember getting a spanking that did not leave a mark for a very short time.

During 1970s in Oklahoma City, integration of races was taking place within the school districts. This was being achieved by transporting some of the white students to the black side of town, and the black students to the white side of town.

One day another boy and I got into a shoving match while in the lunch line. The principal was a big man, who abruptly snatched both of us up, dragging us off to his office. While sitting in front of the office, the other kid, who had evidently been in the principal's office before, started crying uncontrollably; the biggest tears I had ever seen. Well, the principal called in the other kid first and it did not take me long to figure out why he was crying.

When I was next, the principal laid into my butt with a rubber hose. I will go on record as saying using a rubber hose on someone is abusive and a little excessive. That thing left welts on my behind for two weeks. But, I learned my lesson and I never misbehaved in that school again.

If corporal punishment was still in the schools as well as at home, our kids would have more respect for their teachers and parents. I truly believe the learning atmosphere at school would be greatly improved, resulting in students being more focused on learning, rather than being mischievous. It just takes one kid to cross the line and feel the wrath of the paddle to teach the other kids they do not want anything to do with it.

There are lessons in life children need to learn, and sometimes those lessons are going to be a little painful. I guarantee the painful ones are never repeated. I will also tell you I have seen hundreds of inmates in the prison system who were raised under the watered down corporal punishment law of today.

They did not learn these little painful lessons as a child. There was no sense of fear hanging over their head for wrongdoing. Now look at them, sitting in prison learning a much more painful lesson, resulting in the loss of their freedom.

In today's society there seems to be no recourse for bad behavior, thus there is no lesson learned by the child. We all know telling a child or a teenager not to do something results in them doing it anyway. I know this. I have raised three kids who were forewarned not to do various things in life, but they had to find out for themselves. These little lessons usually resulted in me being woke up by a phone call at midnight asking me to come rescue them.

Telling a child to go to their room does not solve anything. It just gets them out of your hair for the moment. Telling them they did something wrong will usually result in them thinking, "Yeah, Mom, whatever," because they do not respect their parents or fear them to a certain degree.

But if little Johnny had experienced his mother's wooden spoon a few times growing up, maybe later in life when mom told him not to do something, he might listen to her warning and not do it. He might think twice about going against mom's word knowing the wood spoon was not far away.

Don't take me wrong. I will not stand for abusing children. As a matter of fact I despise anyone who is sick enough to do injury to a child, and I will be the first to put a stop to it. But children need discipline, such as a little swat on the behind in public, even if it leaves a temporary mark. This is not abuse.

After working in a prison for 25 years, I have learned that those who break rules such as abusing another person will continue doing it whether there is a law against it or not. For instance, every state has laws against carrying a firearm in public. Most states say you have to have a concealed weapon permit, which means the state and federal government will do a background investigation on the person.

Do you really believe criminals go out and get permits to carry a weapon? No, they do not. Matter of fact, they buy stolen guns so the guns will not be traced back to them after using them in a crime. Criminal or mentally ill people do not care about laws, and if you think eliminating corporal punishment will stop abuse, then you are greatly mistaken.

The person who abuses his wife by hitting her is the same person who will abuse a child. The impulse to hurt another person out of rage is an anger related mental illness. Banning corporal punishment will not stop an ill person from abusing his or her child.

The only thing that will stop that person from hurting another individual is to remove them from society permanently, because if he or she comes back it will start all over again. All it takes is one thing to trigger them and they will be back to their same old self.

A lot of mental health professionals believe most people went down a bad road because they were abused as a child. Maybe in some cases this is true, but a large portion of the cases are the opposite. You are looking at criminals who raised themselves as a child, and were allowed to be individuals without any support factors at home. The parents of these criminals allowed them to run wild in the streets at all hours of the day and night, while they basically lived by their own set of rules. The parents of these young criminals have forgotten one of Dr. Spock's main rules, and that is show your child a lot of love, affection and support, which is what is needed to become a well rounded individual.

The baby boomer generation grasped Dr. Spock's theories, along with key psychiatrists who believed spanking a child creates an emotionally unbalanced person. I believe the lack of discipline at home has evolved a generation of emotionally unbalanced children who fear no one. They feel neglected by their parents because they did not love them enough to step in and stop them from doing wrong, while hanging out with the bad element. They feel let down that no one cared enough to teach them right from wrong.

We are now into the third generation of these hands-off theories, which were evolved by psychiatrists trying to make a name for themselves, and these undisciplined children are now parents. This generation believes being on entitlement programs like welfare is a job.

They are perfectly happy walking everywhere they go. Giving birth to children as fast as they can, not because they love them, but rather because it means they will receive a higher welfare check.

The statement I just made is very real. It is not unusual for a young teenage girl who was raised on the welfare system to be very excited about finding out she is pregnant. They are not excited because they are bringing in a new life into the world. They are excited because they will start receiving their own welfare check in the mail. Welfare has become a way of life for many people. They look at it as being a job, and then there are so many hardworking people out there who are barely making it in life, having to support this attitude.

You might think I do not have a lot of faith in psychiatrists. I have met a lot over the years working in the prison system. Some who I have met were excellent professionals and then there were those who I believed to be more nuttier than the patients they were assigned to help.

Prominent individuals involved in the mental health field have influenced federal and state level lawmakers to water down corporal punishment laws over the years. They have convinced lawmakers this is the fix to stop our youth from being abused and stop them from acting out violently. They sold their theory that spanking children was abusive and disrupting their mental balance.

I do agree abusing kids is wrong, but I learned a long time ago that a person who abuses someone else is mentally disturbed and whether corporal punishment is banned or not, they will continue to abuse their children. The only way to help those kids will be to take them away from their abusive parents.

In 1967, New Jersey became the first state to abolish corporal punishment in its school system, followed by Massachusetts in 1974. Now there are very few states that allow spanking in their school systems across the nation.

Parents as well as educators in the public school systems no longer have the right to discipline a child by means of spanking, a tool used for centuries to teach children right from wrong, while reinforcing that there is consequences for bad behavior.

The teachers today may not want the responsibility of disciplining a child, now that corporal punishment has been gone so long. But corporal punishment has been replaced with a new trend in our school systems. It is called teachers carrying concealed weapons to the classroom. Now tell me our youth is not out of control.

Spanking a child in California as well as other states in the nation is almost extinct. Most states have not gone as far as to outlaw spanking, but if you leave a mark on their little behind, it might buy you a one way trip to jail. The kids know this. It is drilled into their heads in school. They are taught if your parents spank you and leave a mark that is abuse and they should report it.

Our teachers today our teaching the state laws to the kids, which has put a scare into parents at home, resulting in a major lack of discipline being enforced. Let's face it, our children love us, but they have to have a little fear in the back of their minds about what mom and dad are going to do to them when they find out they have mis-behaved.

I remember one day my daughter had done something very wrong. She was about ten at the time. She knew very well she was in trouble, so the first thing she said to me was, "You cannot spank me, the teachers said so and if you do all I have to do is let them know."

Well, needless to say I was not planning on spanking her at that time, but after that act of defiance I gave her a swat. To this day she still laughs about those spankings and states it was the best thing for her.

Parenting rights are being taken away little by little in regards to disciplining their children. This has left California and other states in the situation of having a large population of aggressive juveniles who under the old corporal punishment laws would have learned at a young age, if they got out of line, there would be a price to be paid.

Now our kids go to school at a very young age with guns and knives. It is not uncommon to hear about a student going in and shooting up their school, killing their fellow classmates because they have a point to make and they want the whole world to know they are unhappy. You have to wonder if parents were allowed to spank their kids and enforce good morals, if these shootings would slow down or not happen at all.

California is a very liberal state. There is such a problem with aggressive juvenile offenders, and they are being tried as adults for certain crimes. We have adult prisoners who do not understand right from wrong. They believe the set of rules they have established for themselves to follow are the only rules that matter. It is not uncommon for them to call mommy or daddy when they get in trouble at the prison to let them know they are being unfairly treated.

Now in some cases these are the same people who failed them in the first place with no discipline at home. The same people who allowed them to hang out with the bad element and do whatever they wanted. The same people who allowed them to establish their own standards to live by.

The phone calls are always the same. I did nothing wrong and the Correctional Officers beat me up. He failed to tell his parents he spit in the officer's face or was caught stabbing another inmate and he refused to stop.

In the end here come all the liberal politicians along with every liberal lawyer who has made it their job to weaken every aspect of corporal punishment, wanting a full investigation and someone fired. The lawyers also know they will make a lot of money from the state.

I cannot keep from thinking that if corporal punishment was still in place at home as well as in the school systems, a lot of these kids could have been saved from the juvenile and prison system.

Before I move forward I think it would be unfair to those parents who did the best job they could with their young adult who became a criminal. There are those cases where parents go above and beyond the call of duty to ensure their children do not go down the wrong path in life. But no matter how hard they tried, their child chose to sneak out at night to hang out with the wrong crowd. They made it a point to do the opposite of what their parents had taught them.

Psychiatrists interview inmates incarcerated in prison and always ask them the same question, "Were you abused as a child?" I have been around criminals long enough to know one thing for certain, they will never take responsibility for their own actions. The reason they did the crime was because they were abused as a child or they did not do the crime, or they were set up by the police.

Very few inmates will stand up like a man and say, "I am guilty for the crime I have committed and I deserve to be locked away for such crime." I have interviewed hundreds of inmate while assigned as a gang investigator. The conversation always ends the same, "I am not guilty of the crime I am incarcerated for," or "They unjustly sentenced me." But I never once heard an inmate tell me he committed a crime because his parents spanked him.

According to the Federal Bureau of Investigation, law enforcement agencies in 1992 made 2.3 million arrests of persons below the age of 18. Juveniles were involved in 15% of murder arrests,

16% of forcible rape, 26% of robbery, 15% of aggravated assault, 34% of burglary, 44% of motor vehicle theft, 23% of weapon violations, and 23% of drug law violation arrests.

The report went on to indicate between 1988 and 1992, the total number of juvenile arrests increased by 11%, compared to a 6% increase for adults. The increase of murders conducted by juveniles was 51%, compared to a 9% increase in the number of adults arrested for murder.

In 2009, murder offenses fell sharply with juvenile offenders, but drug related offenses went up. In 2011, the federal government reported the adult population across the nation housed in prison was about 6,977,700 offenders by the end of the year.

Maybe some of these young adults could have been productive citizens if the corporal punishment laws had not been watered down or removed, and good parents were not afraid to discipline and take control of their children. Undoubtedly even some of these young adults would have went on to a life of crime, going against their parents' wishes by becoming addicted to drugs and falling victim to outside influences.

# CHAPTER 6
## CHILD ABUSE AND NEGLECT

Child abuse is most certainly a sad situation. As I have already stated, I cannot accept nor will I stand for an adult hurting a child. A child is so innocent by nature and unable to take care of themselves for a very long period of time. Our job as parents is to protect our children from harm caused by those outside of the family structure, as well as harm from those within the family structure.

Abuse comes in many forms but always has the same impact. It destroys a child's ability to develop like a normal person. We are going to start out this segment by defining child abuse. "Child abuse is considered the physical, sexual or emotional maltreatment or neglect of a child."

Abuse can occur in many places such as at home, organizations your child takes part in, day-care and many other places a child is left alone with an adult or minor. It has been a high priority to wipe out child abuse across the nation. Even though there are laws put in place to ward off abusive treatment of children the trend still surfaces.

People who commit abuse of a child come from many walks of life and/or social statuses. They may be a doctor, lawyer, law enforcement, religious figures or even someone living on the bad side of town who is poor. A person that commits abuse has a mental illness. They act out to hurt other people whether it be physically or emotionally without thinking about how they are affecting the targeted person.

These acts of abuse if not stopped can result in serious physical or emotional harm , or even death. There was a recent scenario where a young father physically abused his two-month-old baby. He was turned in by the mother of the child for child abuse and received anger management classes. Once the therapist felt he was well enough he was rejoined with his family. It was not long before his old tendencies surfaced again and he physically abused his young baby, resulting in the child's death.

As I said earlier, I feel being an abusive person stems from some type of mental illness. A lot of people who have anger problems go through the steps of therapy because they have to, due to getting into trouble. Many times they know they have done wrong and they try to suppress the anger inside of them. Unfortunately, in many cases something triggers their anger again and thcy revert back to being the person they were when they got into trouble originally.

Physical abuse stems from angry aggression unleashed on a child. If not stopped, it can lead to serious injury or death. When a child ends up in a medical facility to be treated for bruises, scratches or broken bones, the medical staff are obligated to figure out how that child became injured.

They will start talking with the parents and eventually end with talking to the child. This is done to see if they can find any evidence of abuse. Unfortunately children love their parents very much and do not want to hurt them in any way by telling the truth, resulting in them lying or going along with a fake story created to cover the truth. Children love their parents so much they do not want to see them in trouble.

You have to ask yourself; why would an adult allow themselves or someone else to hurt a child who loves them so much they are willing to protect them by covering up their action? Actions that may have resulted in a broken leg, due to the abuser failing to control their anger.

It is not uncommon for a child who lives with an abusive parent to end up in the hospital multiple times with serious injuries. It seems sometimes the only way to fix the issue is to permanently remove that abusive adult from the child's life.

Psychological abuse is considered emotional abuse. It can come in many forms such as yelling, being verbally abusive, saying things designed to make them feel unworthy, not good enough or not physically attractive enough.

This type of abuse is meant to beat a person down emotionally, so the abuser feels like they are in power or full control. It is not unlike being a bully, and feeling the sense of being in full control of those who surround them.

The impact on a child's emotional state can be great. It can cause severe depression and an increased nervous state, especially when in the company of the abuser. If you know the truth, the adult who verbally abuses a child has probably been a bully his or her whole life and gets enjoyment out of controlling and suppressing other people.

Emotional abuse can also stem from leaving a child in their crib or in a dark room for long periods of time. Such abuse comes from parents who stay up late at night and then decide it is alright to sleep until noon. These parent figures maybe asleep, but a child's normal wake up time is usually by early morning. So while the parent figure is laying in bed sleeping, the child is sitting in a dark room awake for long hours at a time.

Babies and toddlers need stimulation. If they are confined to their crib in the dark, they are not receiving stimulation, but rather their mind is being suppressed and not given the opportunity to grow. This type of abuse can lead to emotional problems that may not be reversible down the road.

these problems include not being able to interact with other kids without fighting, or going into deep thoughts about something, such as watching a TV show, and even though you are calling their name, they seem to have everything blocked out of their world except that show they are watching. They can become easily upset, resulting in crying bouts and in some cases violent reactions toward other people.

Yes, doing this to your child is abuse. Just because you stayed up late and want to sleep in, which seems to be a trend with a lot of young people these days, you have an obligation to get up and get your child's day started early. Your baby or toddler needs your stimulation, and they need you for safety. Sitting in a dark room makes a person feel like their life is empty. It creates loneliness and in some cases probably is very scary to an infant or toddler.

Another thing you need to think about, these tactics have been used across the world to impose punishment and break the will of another person. What is keeping your toddler from thinking they are being punished or no one cares about them? This type of abuse happening over long periods of time can cause a child's emotional state to break down.

Neglect or maltreatment is seen every day in society. It has not been uncommon for me to witness a child not much older than six walking down a busy neighborhood street, all alone without an adult figure with them. When I see this I have to ask myself, where are their parents? My kids while growing up were not even allowed to be out by the street. When they played outside they played in the back yard or at least had to stay close to the house so we could see them.

As a parent when my children were very young it was my job to do their thinking for them, to ensure they were safe from harm. I had to be concerned with them being abducted or even getting run over by a car. Today it seems like a lot of parents do not think of these issues or they just believe it will never happen to their child. The reality is it can happen to any child and it happens every day of the week.

I was at my granddaughter's kindergarten function the other day. After the function was over the parents were given an opportunity to visit with their child. My wife and I were leaving the auditorium and a parent standing in the door looked at us saying, "Hey, someone's infant is walking around in the parking lot."

The parental safety side of me kicked in and I went outside searching for this infant. Sure enough, there was a toddler in the parking lot sitting on the ground against a fence in front of some parked cars. As I approached him and he was crying because he realized he was lost. After taking a moment to reassure him he was going to be alright, I carried him back inside the auditorium where I was met by his father. He approached his child by saying "Don't be wandering off." He grabbed the toddler by the hand and away they went.

This situation could have ended really badly. As a parent you need to understand children get easily distracted and are very adventurous. When they are young, they do not think about what they are doing or the repercussions for doing it. In this case the child wandered off because the parent was not watching him well enough. The parent did not even know he was missing until we brought him back inside. When a child is this young they assume they're always within their parent's safety net wherever they go.

As a parent, it is your job to keep track of them and know at all times where they are and what they are doing. As I said earlier, when it comes to safety, you have to do their thinking for them.

In this scenario I just described there were two errors made. The first was a father who let himself get so preoccupied to the point he lost track of his toddler. The second mistake was made by the parent standing in the door. Too many people do not want to step forward and take control of a situation. Instead they will tell someone else about what is going on in hope that they will take control.

When it comes to a toddler or infant in danger, you get moving. There is no time to alert someone else. This situation could have ended with that toddler being abducted, wandering off and getting completely lost or being run over in a very busy parking lot. And yes, if you are wondering, not watching your child and allowing them to place themselves in a situation that can cause them harm is a form of neglect.

Neglect is probably the most prominent form of child abuse. It comes in so many forms, such as leaving a child at home alone at too young of an age, not feeding them and clothing them properly, not getting them medical treatment when needed and allowing them to run in the streets at all hours of the day and night.

Once your neglect causes harm to a child, it becomes maltreatment. Maltreatment occurs when you allow a child to get hurt or you place them in a situation that is likely to get them hurt. Please watch your kids, make sure they are safe, and make sure they are not around the wrong people or influences.

Let us talk a little about sexual abuse. Sexual abuse occurs when an adult or older adolescent participates in a sexual act with a child, such as fondling or sexual penetration for their own sexual stimulation and gratification. It can even include exposing one's genitals or showing pornography to a child.

Before we get started talking about this, I want to discuss something I have observed in the prison setting that was very prominent. That which I am speaking of is elderly people being convicted of child molestation or sexual abuse and being placed in prison setting.

After observing so many elderly men coming into the prison system, I asked my wife who is a nurse why she thought this was so prominent. She told me something that made a lot of sense. A lot of the times elderly people's mental state reverts back to the time when they were children themselves. This results in them being attracted to young children. In the end they start fondling or in some cases even have sex with a child.

We all have elderly family members who come in contact with our children. I want you to remember what we have just talked about concerning dementia and how it can impact a family member's mind. If you have a family member who suffers from dementia, then it does not hurt to keep a good eye on your young children, without making it evident you are doing so. That is the best way to ensure something does not happen to them that will affect your whole family.

Sexual assault whether it is on an adult or a child has a long lasting impact on that person's life. I often think about why sexual assaults have such a long lasting effect on adults, considering most adults are very sexually active.

The only thing I can attribute the long term effects to is the emotional destruction the victim suffers due to the sexual act being committed against them without their consent. Such an act is considered degrading, brings on severe anger, and it is a defining act of betrayal that leaves a long term sense of distrust in other people.

With children, sexual abuse brings on a lot of emotional side effects. Sometimes the victim bears the burden of guilt and often blames themselves for the sexual act. Nightmares are associated with such abuse, bringing on the reenactment of the act committed against them.

It is not unusual for the child to not have trust for adults of the opposite sex due to the assault. In the end they can have low self esteem, personality disorders, suicidal tendencies and many more side effects.

More times than not the person who sexually assaults a child is someone they know. It can be a father, mother, brother, sister, cousin or close friend of the family. In a lot of the cases it is a juvenile who is not thinking rationally about the impact the assault is going to have on the child's life as well as their own.

Psychological abuse can occur when a child is consistently yelled at or humiliated. This type of abuse comes from a person who likes to ridicule other people with a very aggressive, rude attitude. They control their victims by calling them names or destroying their personal belongings, even including killing pets that the child is very close to.

They might make demands upon a child fully knowing the child is unable to fulfill their wishes, utilizing this situation to criticize them in a harsh manner. In the end the child distances themselves from other people, thinking they are not as smart as others who surround them. They can become aggressive due to constantly being beat down emotionally.

In the end no matter what type of child abuse is imposed on a child, it makes them have social development problems throughout their life. these development issues were imposed on them by another person who may be suffering from sort of mental illness. If your child is being abused in any manner, take action. Do not try to cover the abuse up in the hope that it will go away. I want you to understand it will not go away until someone steps in and puts a stop to it.

# CHAPTER 7
## YOUTH BLINDED BY MEDIA ILLUSIONS

Our children today live in a brainwashed and blinded atmosphere created by the entertainment industry (TV). Good clean family entertainment has been replaced by reality TV, which defies every aspect of moral teaching we have tried to instill into our children.

The entertainment industry says if you don't like it, don't let your children watch it. I say it is time for the entertainment industry to grow up and become responsible adults. It's time for them to remember the morals they were taught as a child. And furthermore, it is time for them to hold themselves accountable for what our children are exposed to via their programs, and not put profit making ahead of what is good moral entertainment. I will go on record as saying not all reality shows are bad, but I would like to see the industry be more selective when choosing future shows.

It seems like the entertainment industry hangs their hat on the old phrase, "Money talks and bullshit walks," which has become their bottom line. In other words, your children are expendable if there is a profit to be made.

I do agree that as a parent it is your responsibility to monitor what your children watch on TV.

But when good family type shows are being replaced more and more every day with reality TV, it makes it difficult to find a decent show that a child can watch and does not teach them negative behavior traits.

The television networks and movie industry seem to feed on violence and misconduct. They go to great lengths to pay attention to what our emotionally starved youth want in their fantasy world by supplying them with role models to meet their needs. If it is violence they crave, it is violence they will get. If they are looking for a role model who is violent but a good guy, then that is what we will create. We all have a little curiosity and renegade in us and that is what the entertainment industry is betting on to attract the youth to their movies.

Today's reality shows portray juvenile kids fighting and bickering through the whole show and our kids are glued to the TV taking in every word they are saying, laughing like it is Comedy Central. Well this type of reaction is what the industry is hoping for.

The saddest thing about it is the young adults today in their late twenties and early thirties like watching this stuff as much as their young kids do. I do not know if it's because they enjoy looking at the young participants on the shows or if they are fascinated by how people can have such bad morals.

There were shows out there like *Terra Nova*, which was a big hit with adults aged 18 to 43. After one season it was canceled by Fox not because of its ratings it had an average of 7.2 million tuned in to each episode. It came down to cost and it did not fit the trend of the industry. You know, the reality industry. It does not cost much to have juvenile delinquents sitting across from each other on a couch, telling the other person to speak to the hand.

What happened to the good old days, when a child came home from school and looked forward to seeing shows like *the Monsters, The Three Stooges, The Addams Family, Andy Griffith* or *Dennis the Menace*. Well maybe not Dennis the Menace, we have enough teenage menaces out in society. Sure these shows did not teach our kids anything, but they also did not harm them in any way. TV leaves a big impression on our youth, and the industry needs to be role models, and take this into consideration when they are looking for a new program to put on the air.

In the '60s and '70s, when a person was shot in a movie or on a TV show, right before it occurred the camera would move away from the violent scene, leaving it to the viewers' imagination what just occurred. Today, watch out. You get to see heads blow off, brains blowing out of the back of the skull in slow motion as the bullet exits, and don't forget my favorite the blood spatter against the wall in real time.

In 1999, the federal government conducted a study indicating by the time a child reaches the age of 18, he or she will have seen 200,000 dramatized acts of violence and 40,000 dramatized murders. Through this exposure, some troubled children develop a taste for violence.

Have you ever wondered how a 10 year old can take a handgun and kill another child with ease? This is due to them seeing it on TV every day.

Their parents rent movies which show a dozen people being explicitly killed. It happens because they have become hardened and desensitized to the aftermath of death.

They have become hardened inside to the point they do not fear what it would be like to shoot someone. All of us have what it takes to kill another person, but fear stops 95% of us from acting on that ability. Fear and all the sickening elements of shooting another human have been exposed to these children over and over on TV, to the point it no longer bothers them.

Since 1997 there has been so many shootings involving young kids and young adults. The list is extensive. The following is just a handful of trage-dies which have occurred across the nation:

*October 1, 1997, Luke Woodham 16, from Pearl, Mississippi fatally shot two students and wound-ed seven others after stabbing his mother to death.*

*December 1, 1997,Michael Carneal 14, shot an killed three students and also wounded five others at a High School in West Paducah, Kentucky.*

*March 24, 1998, Andrew Golden, 11 and Michael Johnson, 13, shot and killed four girls and a teach-er, leaving 10 others wounded at Jonesboro, Ar-kansas.*

*May 21, 1998, Kip Kinkel, 17, shot and killed two teenagers and wounded 20 other kids at Spring-field, Oregon after he had shot and killed his par-ents.*

Some people say we need more government regulations imposed on the entertainment indus-try. I do not believe government regulations are the answer, because all kinds of elements play into that equation things that religion minded politicians want, animal activist want, green minded activist want, and so forth. The list will go on. But I do believe we need to take the movie and TV industry back to a more moral state of time in our history. The current ratings indicate the following age group watch reality TV: 26% teenagers, 30% adults in their thirties, 12% over 50, and 31% don't watch it at all.

The video games our children and young adults play today have them glued to their seats to the point they do not want to eat. Young adults would rather play Nintendo or Xbox than help their wife with the kids or even go to work to support their family. It seems like these games are created in a manner to addict the player, putting them in a trance state of mind, ensuring they spend long hours there and do not leave. The games of today have far surpassed Pac-Man and Mario Brothers, they appear to be more based on thrill seeking.

The video games our kids play have put the final touch on whether a person can take another person's life or not. Combine the viewing of graphic murder movies containing explicit details with interactive video games, and you have kids who are being groomed to become the ultimate killing machine. All this free training takes place in the convenience of their living room. Now what this adds up to is a home version of a trained hit man.

Now do I believe all kids will be affected like this? No, I do not. But what about those children who are emotionally unbalanced? What about the kids who are unbalanced and no one has observed those traits in them as of yet? These are the kids who may act on what they are observing.

Youth violence has grown in America at an alarming rate. Statistics show they have a remarkable ability to fire a handgun with accuracy, even if they have never shot one before. This accuracy is due to the video games they are playing, which are very interactive. When playing these games it is as though you are in a simulator, being placed in real life situations. The games teach these young kids how to hold a gun properly, and how to squeeze the trigger off with accuracy. Unfortunately the games do not teach them about the consequences of killing another person.

*On April 20, 1999, Eric Harris, 18, and Dylan Klebold, 17, entered into the Columbine High School in Littleton, Colorado, and opened fire on the students, killing 12 kids and wounded 26 others.*

*On March 5, 2001, Charles Williams, 15, killed two students and wounded 13 others at Santana High School in Santee, California.*

*On March 21, 2005, Jefferey Weise, 16, entered into the Red Lake Indian Reservation High School, shooting and killing five classmates, a security guard and a teacher.*

You might say that is crazy, but let's take a look at what types of training the military and law enforcement undergo to prepare them to kill another human in the line of duty. It is a gradual training, or some may call it mind altering. The internal hardening of the person's soul to have the ability to kill instinctively if necessary.

When undergoing such training, it is reinforced that it is either you or them. Just like in the video games, if you get killed the game is over. You are doing it to protect your country or the public. During this type of training the student will end up seeing explicit material to prepare them for the aftermath, the emotions they will feel, should they have to kill someone. This is called the hardening of the inner soul and is similar to the explicit material our kids are watching on TV today.

And finally you are put through shoot and no-shoot scenarios. These scenarios do not give the trainee much time to think. They are put together in a manner to exercise the trainee's instinctive reaction time.

Let's review this. Our kids seeing explicit death related material on TV day in and day out, the lessons taught to them by interactive video games, training them to pull the trigger instinctively on another person, and then finally the survival reinforcement, it is either them or you. This is similar to a stick of dynamite lying around. The dynamite by itself is fairly harmless, but when you add the blasting cap, it becomes deadly.

The military and some law enforcement agencies utilize video simulators to put their people through real life threatening situations. The military puts their fighter pilots in video simulators to show them what it feels like to be in a dog fight with an enemy plane. A lot of times they are no-win scenarios, to teach the pilot they may die.

The end result of all this is similar to the video games our children play today. Unfortunately, some of the kids may be emotionally unstable and end up going down the wrong path. Sadly, they may end up killing another person and living behind prison walls because they became hardened enough to kill the neighbor kid over an argument.

Hey, here is a scenario we've been hearing a lot about in the news the last few years. A teenager walks into a school, shooting 20 or more students who were once their playmates growing up, just to make a statement and get some attention.

*April 16, 2007, Seung-Hui Cho, 23, fatally shot 32 people in a dorm and a class at Virginia Tech in Blacksburg.*

*February 14, 2008, Steven Kazmierczak, 27, opened fire in a lecture hall at Northern Illinois University, killing 5 students and wounding 21 others.*

*February 27, 2012, Police charged T.J. Lane, 17, with shooting and killing three students in a high school cafeteria in Chardin, Ohio.*

Military psychologists, whose job is to deal with battle fatigue and soldiers coming home unstable from the war, has forewarned in their writings that the violent video games of today in conjunction with the explicit violence in movies has conditioned our youth to become violent.

Today's entertainment and interactive video game industry have desensitized our children to violent acts, and are leading their young minds into believing brutality is an acceptable part of life. The movies portray characters showing dominance and the hurting of other people as being powerful. For children who cannot separate reality from fiction, this could become very dangerous.

There have been many studies done over the years by various groups indicating the violence on TV, in conjunction with violent video games, appears to be having a mind altering affect on our kids, while hardening them to be violent individuals. The bottom line is that their outside influences are teaching them to hurt and kill.

Our children are making role models out of violent characters on TV and in the movies. Look at the Batman movies. They did not remind me of the original Batman series ran in the 1960s. The movies have been made so highly sadistic in nature. The characters all seem to be mentally unbalanced, including Batman.

Michael Keaton in 1989 starred in *Batman* and again in 1992 in *Batman Returns*. Keaton in an interview vowed never to do another Batman movie, because being in that character for such long periods of time was very emotionally hard on his mental status. The Batman movies have come under fire by outside groups because of the high level of violence portrayed in them, along with the graphic sex scenes.

*On July 20, 2012, during the premier of the Batman movie, Dark Knight Rises, gunman James Holmes entered into the Century 16 movie theater in Aurora, Colorado, armed with an assault rifle, a shotgun and handguns. Holmes started his attack by dispersing teargas canisters, then opened fire, killing 12 moviegoers.*

*After Holmes was arrested in the parking lot of the theater, he was found to have dyed his hair part orange and part red. When asked who he was supposed be, he stated he was the Joker. Later during a search of Holmes' apartment, a Batman mask was recovered.*

Children mimic what they see adults do. If you as a parent slip every once in a while with a foul word in front of your young children, guess what your children will be saying next. They do not know what the word means, but it has to be OK because mom or dad said it, and they struggle to be just like their parents.

When I was a young parent and first joined the department, being around criminals all day all I heard was constant profanity. Unknowingly my own vocabulary became more and more filled with needless profane words. One day my family and I were visiting my elder aunt and my two young daughters (age four and five) were on the carport with my aunt riding their tricycles, when all of a sudden my aunt yelled for me to come to her.

She said, "Weldon, have you been cussing in front of these children?" Of course I said no, but she knew better. She went on to tell me how they were riding their bikes singing the Fuc..... song they had made up. I thought to myself there is no way to squirm out of this mess. The lesson is children mimic what role models say and do. If the role model does it or says it, it must be OK.

I believe children who kill others are mentally unstable. They were either born with a mental disorder or they acquired it growing up as their minds were developing. Children are easily influenced by their environment and in some cases all it takes is one shocking event to take place in their lives to put them over the edge, such as a death of a parent or divorce.

Children will attempt to copy others. Unstable children with a violent side will attempt to mimic violent role models who they have come to admire. After the Columbine shooting, copycat attempts by other unstable teens were seen around the country. Those attempting to copy this shooting tried to pull it off on a much grander scale. The social network was ridden with a number of mentally unstable kids expressing admiration for the two suicidal shooters.

Is there a solution to this problem? Yes, but it starts at home. You as a parent have to be selective about what types of entertainment your children are raised on. You cannot depend on the entertainment industry to clean up its act, because they are out to make money.

That means you as a parent will have to sacrifice the things you like to do or watch, at least when the kids are around. Because if it is OK for you, you're mimicking child will believe it is OK for them. No more killing type movies in front of your children. No more interactive violent video games, because if it is good for you, it is OK for the child.

Children can only handle certain amounts of violence at different age levels growing up. Separating behavior actions such as right from wrong, acceptable and unacceptable come at different levels of the maturing process. Children must be taught there are consequences for those who act out with violence.

*April 2, 2012, One Goh, killed seven people at the California Christian University because he was angry over his tuition cost.*

*December 15, 2012, Adam Lanza, 20, shot and killed his mother at home, then preceded to Sandy Hook Elementary School, Newtown Connecticut, where he shot and killed 25 students and faculty.*

Unlike in the movies, in a real life situation, if a police officer had shot and killed 12 criminals in a twelve-hour period and blew up half the town in the process, he would not be a hero of the moment. The first thing the city administration would do is tell the police department to take the officer's gun and badge, then instruct him he was on administrative leave for several weeks pending an investigation into his actions. This is not exactly how it is portrayed in the movies.

There is a great difference between how an adult and a child distinguish between fantasy and reality. Distinguishing between the two is a much more difficult task for a child. For instance, your beautiful two-year-old daughter, who you admire so much, walks up to your older child and hits her with her hand while you're not looking. This is your child's first act of violence. Did you teach it to them, maybe by playing little soft hitting games? The greater chance is they saw it on TV, watching their favorite cartoon.

Every element that our children come in contact with is very impressionable upon them. It can be a positive impact or a negative impact in their growing up. We all like to blow raspberries and nibble on our baby's belly, but we our reinforcing biting traits. This will come later down the road in the form of a way to defend or compete with another child.

Even though the things our kids find entertaining, such as the media and the gaming industry, have a negative impact on them, they are not solely at blame, and it is our job to set our child's environment up for them. Children are not born bad, we make them that way. We have to make decisions for them early in life, teaching them right from wrong and instilling morals and consequence for bad actions.

Those of us who try really hard to instill morals into our kids, are having to battle the outside elements, which appear to be constantly on the attack. It's hard enough today to be a single parent, or parents who both have to work to support the household. We do not need outside distractions such as TV programs or games that are put together in bad taste, to tear down what we are building.

All the violent acts of teenagers have become prominent in the news today and should be a message to parents that the current way of raising children is not working. It is time for parents to get politically involved to help persuade politicians to clean up the negative environment our children are being influenced by.

# CHAPTER 8
## ALPHA COMPLEX

In this chapter we are going to discuss the alpha complex. We will discuss how it fits into the parenting role at home and how it affects our children and their social life. And we will discuss how the parent must be a good alpha role model.

The alpha complex is similar to the alpha animal complex. Let's say you have three dogs in your back yard. There will always be one dominant dog out of the three. There will be an established pecking order put in place, in which the dominant dog leads the pack.

Let's say you put one dish of food out for your dogs to eat out of. If you watch closely, an established pecking order will unfold before your eyes. The alpha dog will be allowed to eat first, the next dominant dog will eat second and so on.

You might say the male dog will always be the alpha dog, but that is not always the way it unfolds. There have been times I have seen female dogs, which were very aggressive, take on the role of the alpha dog. It is based on their aggressiveness, strength, and their ability to think faster than those who surround them.

This is not unlike the alpha role that evolves in a child's peer group. The same traits play a major role in establishing the pecking order of a group. The child that is the biggest or the strongest , with the ability to think fast on their feet, a lot of the times takes over as the leader. Unfortunately a lot of these kids have not been taught good morals and values.

Related to our parenting skills, the alpha complex takes its own role. With our children, the parents must be the alpha personality of the household, the stronger personality, the faster thinker, bigger in stature and most important. You must be a leader for your children with good morals and values. If parents do not take on the alpha responsibilities of parenting, then you end up with a child who takes on the trait in your place, and the household becomes filled with mass confusion.

The end result is the child is unruly, telling you no when you ask them to do something. Telling you to stop when you grab their hand. The child has observed a lack of leadership from its parents and as the child's mind matures it assumes the alpha role. The alpha role is established already at birth, when the child first sees their mother and father. Once they recognize that you are their parents, they look to you for protection, guidance, comfort, and leadership.

But when you fail to teach your child and stimulate its mind as it grows, teaching simple things such as right from wrong, they start running wild and basically being an individual raising themselves with their own set of rules. If this is not corrected you will gradually lose the role as the alpha in the family.

I see it every day when I go out in public, parents trying to correct their children who are being defiant and the child tells them "no." Another scenario I have seen many times in the store, is the child is running wild through the store, getting into everything, and the parent is just ignoring their actions. In this case the parents have done little to raise their child and have given up.

You never give up. You brought that child into the world, and it is your responsibility to teach them right from wrong, no matter how difficult it might be for you or them. I have observed that same child, who was running wild in the store, lose track of their parents and instantly break into an uncontrollable crying spree out of fear, because they realized they were vulnerable and had lost their security.

That is the opportune moment to talk with them, reinforcing what their bad behavior had caused, and if he or she had done what they were told to do to start with, they would not have had to suffer being frightened. But unfortunately most parents usually just tell them to get over here and that is the end of the conversation.

When my children were toddlers they had to ride in the cart when we were in the store. This was done to control their temptations to grab all those shiny objects that were leaping out at them from the shelves.

When the time came they were old enough to walk alongside the cart, they had to hold onto it at all times. That was the established rule they were taught to abide by. Once they realized that was the way it was going to be, there were no problems.

I do remember one time I failed as a parent in the grocery store. I broke my wife's cardinal rule about the girls being inside the grocery cart at all times. At the time one was three and the other was four. The girls of course did not want to sit in the cart. I told my wife, "Oh, let them walk this time and let's see how they act."

Well that was a big mistake I still hear about even to this day. Up ahead of us was a beautiful pyramid fashioned out of wine bottles. Needless to say, before the girls could be stopped they started chasing each other and one of them grabbed a bottle at the base of the pyramid and the whole thing came crashing to the ground.

Wine was everywhere. Yes, my face was as red as the wine on the floor. I was so embarrassed by my bad decision and my children's actions. I looked at my wife and I could see divorce written all over her face. I never let those kids get out of the cart again until they were 12. No, I am just kidding.

My wife was so angry with me and the experiment was over. The embarrassment was so bad for both of us, I still hear about it to this day, when we have our grandchildren with us in the store. Every once in a while I will look at her asking if we should let the grandchildren walk while we have them in the store. The look I get in return is priceless.

It is important that you as a parent hold the alpha role while raising your children. It is not the child's job to assume the role of raising the parents. If you allow your child to assume that role it will end in chaos. This type of child may end up portraying the qualities of always having to win, while playing, be the best at everything they do, be a know it all.

This type of child's alpha instincts are not being used to take care of others. Instead the alpha instincts are being used to take care of themselves.

To be the alpha parent does not mean you have to be cruel and dominant, it means you need to be loving reassuring, protective and a role model who your child will come to for advice.

The alpha role stretches out into the public. There are two kinds of children out there, the alpha and the followers. It is important that you teach your child to be a leader amongst their peers or they will become a follower in society. It may be in a daycare setting, school or just in your neighborhood. It is important you know at all times what type of children your kids are interacting with, because they learn from each other.

The bottom lines is, if you as a parent live by and teach good morals, show your child how to be kind, but be an effective leader, they themselves will become positive alpha leaders when they are not in your presence.

It is important that there are positive alpha leaders being raised at home. Because when your kids leave to play with their friends there is a pecking order established. You would hope you have taught your child to be a good leader by your example, making sound decisions while surrounding themselves with others whom you would approve of. Doctors have wrote about the alpha child, indicating they come in many different personalities. Some are bossy and prescriptive, dominating and controlling, compelled to take charge, and others are passionate, wanting to help others.

The alpha child is most comfortable when in charge and giving orders. Other alpha children are like mother hens, inclined to take care of others, especially the weak and the wounded, while holding the role of a leader.

The alpha child who is aggressive and a bully wants to establish dominance through exploiting the weaknesses and vulnerability of others. This type of complex has put up a barrier against feelings and responsibilities and only thinks of themselves.

When the child assumes the alpha role in the household they may become non- receptive to being taken care of. In addition, the alpha children tend to be more alarmed about what goes on around them, thus showing signs of anxiety and attention problems. Furthermore, alpha children are also more resistant to taking orders or receiving direction, making them quite difficult for parents to give guidance to.

Our children need a good sound parent-child relationship. They need love from both parents, including tough love. Children today need to feel love and strongly connected to a family unit. They also want to feel safe and protected by their parents. Sometimes when you tell your child "no," they do not like it, but down the road as they mature they will realize you made the right decision and you were only protecting them.

# CHAPTER 9
## OVER PROTECTIVE/ ENABLER PARENT

Researchers have warned that overprotective parenting virtually robs a child of their childhood and identity as an individual. Parents who make their children stay inside and play video games or watch TV, rather than sending them outside to play, are keeping their child from learning social skills. The lack of going outside to play in the sun, combined with very little interaction with other children, threatens the health and emotional well-being of your child.

Parents need to understand when a child goes outside to play with other children, it keeps them active and stimulates their mind while teaching them to get along with other kids.

A lot of children today are overweight due to a lack of exercise. Children used to come home from school and play outside until dark. Now children come home from school, turn on the Xbox or TV, and sit on the couch until it is time to start their homework. The lack of outside playtime and the interactive stimulation of being with other children can lead to mental health related issues and behavioral issues. Researchers indicated there has been a significant decline over the last 15 years concerning children going outside to play.

Schools over the last several years have implemented programs wherein the children have to complete a one-mile run (monthly) to ensure they are getting exercise. I remember when I was a child my mom had to come looking for me because it was getting dark outside and I had not come home from playing.

Another factor about children being outside is the production of vitamin D-3. D-3 is processed from exposure to sunlight. It helps maintain normal blood levels in regards to calcium and phosphorous, and helps the calcium absorb into your bones.

The overprotective parents keep their child by their side at all times. The child is not allowed to venture out too far from the parent figure. They are not allowed to make the little mistakes in life needed to grow into a responsible adult.

This type of parenting figure is usually a single parent. The child is toted around by the parent during the early years of its life and into its teenage years. The parent figure makes all their decisions for them, thus the child does not need to use their own decision making process.

The end result is that the child does not get to learn the feeling of failure, nor do they learn the role of independence or responsibility. When the parent figure makes all the decisions for their child, they are depriving them of experiencing minor failures in life. This is needed to tackle major decision making issues later on as they become adults. My brother once described this type of child as being a walking zombie. Trailing behind the parent figure, waiting on them to make a decision to feed them, take them to the store to buy something. Eventually you have a teenager too lazy to get off the couch.

There are many bad traits instilled in a child raised by an overprotective parent. One trait you see a lot of these days is an adult living at home well into their late twenties. They have a lack of social life because they were not allowed to have a social life as a child. The overprotective parent would not dream of allowing their child go to another kid's house to play or spend the night.

Teenagers raised like this have no self esteem and no drive to socialize with other teens. Thus they have neither friends nor girlfriends or boyfriends as young adults. They do not have any drive to get a job, because in their mind they cannot get far from the parent figure, and they figure the parent will supply them with whatever they need each day.

Sooner or later the parent figure will wake up, tired of their young adult sleeping until noon every day and want them to go out and find their own life and get a job. After being raised like this, the child has no motivation to get out of bed, never mind get a job.

We all want to protect our children. It is essential that we support our children in the things they do and assist them in picking their friends. But it is important that they be allowed to test the waters of life and know what it feels like to make their own decisions even if it results in minor failure.

If you do not allow your child to safely grow up while stubbing their big toe every once in a while, they will become the walking zombie we referred to, following you around everywhere you go, clear into adulthood. As a parent there will be a point in your life when you want your child to leave the nest. This time in your life is when you hope you no longer have to worry about the things your child is doing nor the places they are going.

By this time you have done your best to raise them in a manner where they will make very sound decisions and you hopefully no longer have to worry about them. Well you will always worry about them, because you will always look at them as being your babies. That is part of being a parent.

This point in your life is where you get to finally take care of yourself and not have to be fully responsible for another person. Do the things you want to do, when you want to do them. Do not worry, it won't last long and you will not get bored, because the next wonderful thing that will happen to you is grandchildren and then you will find yourself helping raise them in a lesser role, but nevertheless you still will be helping.

An enabler parent wants everything to be good for their children or young adult. When your child is in a small bind you fix it. When your young adult is running short on money, you are there to help them by pulling out your wallet. We all want to protect our children, but if you do not allow them to feel the sting of being short of money or allow them to figure their way out of a mess, they will not learn from their mistakes.

I believe my wife and I fall under this category. We want the best for our children. We bought each of them their first car. When they came up short on money for bills we do not think twice about shelling out money to them. This is being done because we want them to be protected and succeed in life.

The reality of it is we are holding them back from learning the little lesson of being young adults making their own decisions. We are not letting them learn from their mistakes, because we are always there to bail them out.

As an enabler parent, before you can help your child, you must see the faults in yourself. You must admit to yourself you have been doing more harm than good to your child by being there to bail them out whenever the going gets rough. You must be able to distinguish between enabling and helping. Let's break the difference between the two.

• Helping could be doing a task for someone that they cannot do for themselves, such as giving them money one time to pay a bill.

• Enabling is doing things for someone they are fully capable for doing for themselves, such as giving them money repeatedly to pay bills. If you know deep down in your heart you are an enabler, and you continue to do such acts that create a negative circumstance, you are doing more harm than good for your young adult. You are creating a young adult who will build their existence on taking advantage of other peoples' good will.

# CHAPTER 10
## EDUCATION SYSTEM

The subject of Education has bothered me tremendously for years, or rather the lack of proper education for the children in this nation. I have felt for a very long time that our children have been set up for failure in the current educational system.

The reason I have chosen to put this section in the book is because the education system is supposed to piggyback on the parental teaching at home. It is supposed to build confidence in our children, while preparing them for their next step in life, whether it be college or just entering the work force.

When a child is not succeeding in the classroom, their mental status takes on the makeup of that of a failure. At some point when they are tired of being lost, they just give up and quit. Then the next thing you know they are skipping school and hanging out with the bad element in the neighborhood. Hanging out with the bad element at some point will lead to trouble for the child and parents.

There has been good news coming out of the National Education Center, indicating the dropout rate from 1990, which was 12%, has lowered in 2012 to 7%. This is due in part to laws being enforced to ensure children attend school.

Although the news is better nationally, you have to take into consideration the dropout rate state by state. The Department of Education in California saw an increase in the graduation rate in 2011 to 76%, but still had a 24% rate of non-diploma students, or dropouts, or young adults attending night school to get their high school diploma.

My ideal of a proper education versus what a person with a doctorate considers a proper education are two different things. To me a good education is structured in a manner where enough time is spent on the subject matter that all students understand it, not just a handful of kids in the classroom. When this is achieved then all students participating will feel they are a necessary part of the structured program. No one wants to be looked upon as the dumb kid in the class. All kids want to feel like they have succeeded at the end of the school day.

When students receive grades on their report cards which reflect success, it motivates them to try harder. The old rubber stamp saying he or she is just not applying themselves, sticks out in my mind. My opinion is this statement came about as an excuse for educators to use to cover why their students are failing. The truth of the matter is maybe the child does not understand the curriculum, or maybe the teacher is flat boring them to death. We might even consider the thought that the curriculum has become too advanced for average children to grasp.

My granddaughter is only in second grade, yet she has already brought homework home that represents basic algebra and geometry. Now when I was her age we were still doing basic math, adding, subtracting, division and multiplication. The education system has lost their minds in this country. They are completely skimming over the basics, and jumping into the advanced part of the subjects, thinking this will prepare the student to take advanced subjects in high school. This way of thinking has produced children who cannot even count change back to you at the cash register.

Some educators are fantastic with their students. They come to work with a positive attitude, and bring the best out in their students while interacting with them. Then there are others who seem to believe they're college professors who just put the assignment on the chalkboard, expecting the students to teach themselves. If you are a teacher and this last statement fits you, then you are a bore and you are ripping your school districts off. But worst of all, you are doing a great injustice to those young minds who sit in front of you.

I believe one of the major areas not being taught well enough in schools today is organizational skills, note taking skills and how to prepare for a test etc. A lot of colleges are having to implement programs to teach freshman students these skills, because it was not taught in the lower levels of education.

The United States was once known as the leading, most enterprising, and greatest technological country in the world under the old school system.

It was known for cultivating young minds who were creative and felt the sky was the limit when it came to technology. We were known for an educated work force, which could bring new technology to life. Now I think the only thing the United States is known for is racking up debt, while giving free handouts to countries who do not even especially like us.

Coming out of the 1960s this country was known for its educated population. Other countries strove hard to bring their system up to our standards. I guess that was the beginning of our education system downfall. I believe those at the federal level, knowing other countries were trying to catch up with us, were in fear that one day America would get surpassed.

In the early 1970s the public started hearing more and more about how the United States had to make changes in various areas of the education system to keep up with the rest of the world, especially Asia. The first sign of change started to appear when the federal government wanted to change our measuring system to match the rest of the world.

The United States was using the standard measuring system, which had been in place for a very long time and worked fine us. Other countries were using the metric system, and instead of them changing their ways of measuring to match what the leading technological country was doing, our government leadership decided to change our system from the standard system to the metric system.

In Europe and Asia they were striving to catch up with American technology. I believe there were those at the political level and in the Department of Education who were in fear that the United States was going to lose its technological edge, thus leading to our education system being overhauled.

Our government thought other countries outside of the United States were going to become global powers from their own invented technology, thus overpowering us. What other countries did was outwit us, by ensuring their children received a good education. This would later afford them the opportunity to come to the United States, to attend our major Universities.

You might ask yourself why attending school in the US is so important. Once the foreign students finished college a lot of them went on to obtain high-ranking corporate jobs in prominent technological companies here in the United States. Once hired they gained access to confidential technology and that is when the corporate espionage began.

As the corporations they worked for finished stages of their latest confidential projects, the mole would start filtering the information back to corporations in their homeland or to their government. I want to go on record saying not every foreign student goes on to commit corporate espionage. That would be a ridiculous statement. There have also been plenty of Americans who have done the same thing while working in corporations.

Industrial espionage is most commonly associated with technology heavy industries, including computer software and hardware, biotechnology, aerospace, telecommunications, transportation and engine technology, automobiles, machine tools, energy, materials with coatings and so on. Silicon Valley is known to be one of the world's most targeted areas for espionage, though any industry with information of use to competitors may be a target.

The Department of Education's function is to set policy, administer and coordinate most federal assistance to education, collect data on US schools, and to enforce federal educational laws. The department's mission is to promote student achievement and preparation for global competitiveness by fostering educational excellence and ensuring equal access.

Due to the changes to our education system, the United States' lower levels of education, namely elementary school and high school, are no longer revered as a leading standard to look up to around the globe. I do believe our colleges, especially our medical schools, are revered as some of the finest in the world.

A recent survey was taken by the US Department of education, comparing our children's education test scores between 2007-2011 with other countries' educational test scores. After the comparison was made we proved to be substandard.

In the 1950- 1960s we led the way. We were the role model for the world to follow. Our educational system was an inspiration for other countries to get better. Our elementary schools and high schools actually taught every child in the classroom, not just a few who comprehended what the teacher was talking about.

Today's system is fast paced, and many of our children are lost in the subject material. The curriculum is set up not to go back and gather up those that are lost, but just to sacrifice them for the few who actually understand the material. Now our educational system in place is broke and you cannot go a day without hearing about poor test scores coming out of our schools nationally.

The old statement you cannot leave well enough alone applies here. Over the years the educators of this nation have pushed to inject what were once college level classes into our elementary and high school systems. What were once college prep classes taken at the high school level as elective classes are now considered mandatory in some states, such as algebra.

Algebra has now been introduced at the elementary level, all the way down to the 2nd grade. A friend of mine who was a very good algebra teacher once said if the student does not have a very good understanding of basic mathematics, they will not understand algebra. Today's system skims over all the basics of mathematics, English and history.

Let's go back to why we were the leaders in technology, compared to where we are today. Back in the '50s and '60s, when children were taught in elementary school, they learned the basics of mathematics, reading/writing, history and social studies. When a child entered into high school they had a very strong grip on math (adding, subtraction, multiplying and division), reading/ writing (able to read at grade level and write sentences, understood how a sentence was broken down), history (our children were taught about American history and our forefathers) and social studies (how different cultures function within).

When our children graduated they could read, do basic math fluently, and they had an understanding of how this country was formed and how its infrastructure worked. If there were brilliant kids within the high school setting, they were allowed to take electives such as algebra, trigonometry, advance geometry and so forth.

Back in those days algebra and trigonometry were college level classes. Those that were going into a field which required it would take it at the high school level as an elective class to get a head start on the subject. Those who did not want to go onto college were not required to take it.

Back then when your child entered into the working world, you were pretty assured they had a good grip on adding, subtraction, multiplication and division. They had reading skills and could write a sentence. The end result was that the United States had a strongly educated work force that could meet any challenge.

Those children who excelled in high school and took advanced classes also excelled in college and became future scientists, doctors and inventors. I think this is where we started going wrong. People with higher education started to think if we make all students take advanced courses in high school, then they will all be advanced in their education level and ready for college.

Unfortunately it does not work like that. Not every student, whether you make them take the advance classes or not, will understand the subject matter. Some kids excel in different areas than other kids. When you force a child to learn something he or she does not understand, they will shut down on you, and then you can watch their grades plummet. The biggest problem with this whole equation is a sense of failure starts emerging, which can lead to a whole lot of other problems.

Now we have an even bigger problem emerging today in our school system. Educated administrators have seen fit to give their teachers a curriculum in the classroom that skims over the basics, which is necessary for a child's development. Our children know nothing about American History, they cannot do basic math, and their reading and writing skills are horrific.

*Example: You go to the grocery store. You have a young adult working the cash register in front of you, They go to give you your change after you pay for your items and he or she cannot count your change back to you. Part of this problem is technology. The machine tells them how much money to give back, but what happens if the register has gone haywire and they have to fall back on their basic schooling in mathematics? There's a good chance you will have to count your own change to ensure you received the right amount back.*

The bottom line in the old school system was that we graduated a balanced group of intelligent young adults, with those who could brainstorm a new idea and put it down on paper and a young work force coming out of high school with a basic sound education, which could put their ideas together and make them work. That is why we were a role model for the world.

Today's failed education system is based on survival of the fittest. Our figureheads leading the education departments at the state and federal level just do not get it. Not every child in the classroom setting is going to be a genius. Not every child is going to want to go on to college. The statistics across the nation show that our current education system is a failed system. But nobody is willing to take a step back and say we screwed up, let's scrap this system and go back and piggyback on the old education system and try to make it a little better.

The current system in place is geared up for the highly intelligent kids and all the rest, if they do not get it, are expendable. I once attended a seminar, which promoted a new learning system to teach kids to be more organized in the classroom. The auditorium was full of educators and administrators. The guest speaker stepped on hollow ground when he directed a statement toward all the educators in the audience. He said over the years he had attended a number of graduations from the high school to the college level.

He went on to say he noticed the same trend at both levels on graduation day. The teachers always went out of their way to take pictures with the student who accelerated above all others, but those teachers never went out of their way to take pictures with the kids who barely got by and graduated.

The point he was trying to make to the educators in the audience was it was their job to find ways to make all students accelerate within their classroom. No child gets left behind. The politicians just do not get it, it's not the teachers who are at fault, but rather the educational system and curriculum they have put in place.

There has been a big push to punish the teachers across the nation for the bad testing statistics pouring in. I have even heard the president of the United States chime in on the subject. I am personally tired of hearing government figureheads lashing out at teachers, threatening them with repercussions if their students fail to test well during state level testing. I am sure that there are a few bad teachers out there, but the root of the problem is the upper administration in the education department, all the way to the state and federal level. These administrators need to understand it is not the teachers, it is the educational system and curriculum that they are being forced to teach.

I once sat down with an English teacher who was very frustrated. He indicated the kids he was receiving in high school today were not ready for high school material. He indicated his job to teach basic reading and writing skills has all but been taken over by Comparative Literature (Comp Lit). He said at the beginning of the school year, they go over reading and writing skills and very abruptly go right into Comp Lit. He indicated when it comes time to conduct the state testing on his students, they fail the reading and writing portion miserably because most of them do not understand basic reading and writing.

He said the kids today are lost, and the new targeted subject matter the heads of education have deemed to be more important than the basics skills are making these kids even more lost. Every year our children get tested in the public school systems to see how they are progressing. Each year the results are the same across the nation, bad in all areas.

It is evident that critical thinking skills are overriding the basics of all subject matter. The mentality of our current education system is to turn the screws a little harder on the teachers and maybe the students will do better next year.

I have worked around the youth not only in the high school setting, but also in the prison setting. The national statistics are high in regards to kids skipping school and not graduating high school. The administrators in the education department have geared our teachers up for failure. Our teachers are teaching algebra in the elementary level to kids who do not have a good grip on basic math.

When I was in high school I skipped school one day out of all the years I attended. Today you are lucky to get some kids to school one day out of the week. I believe a lot of this is because the kids are lost in the classroom, which has led to low self esteem. Most of these kids would rather stay home than go to school and look like a dummy in front of their peers.

I do not know about you, but there has not been one day in my life that I have ever needed algebra. I know there are employment fields out there that do use it, but why are we making it mandatory for our youth in elementary and high schools to learn a math they will never use? Why are young adults being made to learn subjects in college that have no bearing whatsoever on the field of study they are going into?

I will tell you why! It is all about money at the college level. They want someone to pay them, whether it is the taxpayer or the individual, for the unnecessary classes. If you cut all the unnecessary required classes out of the course structure to become a doctor, then you would produce a doctor in probably six years versus 10 years. But I do not see that happening because there will be four years worth of money cut out of the college's bank roll.

In the end, the US Department of Education and the state level Department of Education refuse to address the main problem at hand, and that is the education system as a whole is a failure. We need to go back to teaching the basics, and quit trying to keep up with the Asian countries, whose kids go to school year around six days a week.

Yes, they have a higher rate of graduation. Yes, their kids are grasping a higher level of academic courses, but they have a much higher price to pay for failure and a much higher incentive program to succeed in place.

In most cases if a child fails to achieve high academic standards, their families will be shamed by society, and the difference between being allowed to work for a business or working in a low paying job for the rest of their life is determined by their educational success.

Our country was never built on such philosophies, like those in other countries. This country was established in a manner that all can succeed if they wish to do so, no matter the level of education they have achieved.

# CHAPTER 11
## GUNS AT HOME

In today's society gun control seems to be a very hot subject. Politicians as usual are making it a part of their bid for re-election. Guns at home is a very important issue to be discussed, due to the rash amount of shootings taking place across the nation involving children.

Just like the average American family, I too have a collection of guns at home. Being a retired law enforcement officer, I wanted to make it very clear that you, as an adult, are responsible for those weapons being unloaded and secured in a place at home where a child cannot get hold of them.

I also want to inform you that in most states you will be held responsible for your child's actions in regards to discharging one of your weapons. You see it in the news all the time. A child gets their hands on one of their parent's loaded guns and discharges it, resulting in injury to themselves or another child and in some cases death.

Please pay close attention to this. The next thing you will hear or read is that the District Attorney's Office is contemplating filing charges against one or both of the parents for child endangerment and neglect.

It seems the average adult does not contemplate the responsibility of owning a handgun. There is no excuse for a weapon being in a place where a child can reach it. All weapons should be kept unloaded and secured in a safe place, or at least it should have a trigger lock placed on it.

Statistics show in 2008 there were 680 accidental deaths nationwide, followed by 15,000 shooting related injuries. Statistics also indicate there are five children each day injured or killed nationwide by guns. Most of these injuries are due to curiosity. An additional 100 accidental shootings occur each year as the result of cleaning a weapon that was thought to be unloaded.

Due to adult gun owners neglect and lack of responsibility, I truly believe in the very near future there will be a federal law indicating before you will be allowed to purchase any firearms you will be required complete a gun safety course. I also believe most states will enact a law indicating you must own a gun safe, requiring you to keep your guns in it at all times when not in use. Like most laws enacted, it happens because people lack common sense.

Now I know what you are thinking. My child does not know where I keep my loaded handgun. If the gun is within their reach, they will find it. Children see and hear everything you do or say; they are very inquisitive by nature. They see us doing and saying things that we do not realize they have observed or heard.

A lot of people keep handguns on a nightstand next to the bed. Others keep it under their mattress. Does this fit you? Well, if it does, then that means I know where you keep your weapon, so why wouldn't your child? I guarantee you that your child has observed you pulling your weapon out for some reason or another.

Children by nature are very inquisitive. They want to see what dad's toy looks like. You know, the toy they have heard go bang. It is a big person toy, and everybody knows they are a big kid too. They also like showing off their renegade side to their friends, by sneaking them up to your secret hiding spot to show them your gun. Unfortunately this scenario a lot of times ends in a bad way.

You may think just because they are teenagers they have enough sense not to mess with a weapon. Here's a real story that happened to my brother. My brother, who no longer had kids at home, kept a loaded gun in his nightstand. His granddaughter, who was a teenager at the time, and was not raised around guns, was in his room snooping around like so many kids do, wanting to see what kind of good stuff their grandparents had.

While in the room she came across his loaded handgun. He heard noises in the room, so he went in to check it out. He entered just in time to see her cock the hammer on his loaded revolver. He told her to freeze, at which time he took the gun away from her, just in time before she pulled the trigger. He asked her, "What were you thinking?" and she answered, "I did not think it was real."

Listen, this scenario could easily be you one day. If you are going to have guns around the house, then keep them secured. Even if you do not have children, you never know when a child will be in your house. If you have children, buy a gun safe, keep all weapons in it unloaded, and only the parents should know the combination.

Make it a rule all guns, even those you buy for your children to hunt with, stay locked up. Unfortunately, most kids who enter your house are not going to be knowledgeable about weapons, and also it is always the gun which was thought to be unloaded that kills someone.

You might say my kids have been raised around guns their whole life; they all know about gun safety. That might be very true, but their friends probably know very little about guns. And the chances of one of them discharging a weapon are great. Also, when it comes to your own children being around their friends, it is not uncommon for them to want to show off a little by pulling their guns out to show them. This can lead to an accidental discharge.

Now if you are going to have guns around children as they are being raised, it is a good idea to teach them gun safety. They should know how to load and unload a gun safely. They should fully know a gun is meant for only one thing, and that is to kill. They should be taught to never handle a gun unless they are with you. You should also teach them should their friends pull out a firearm in their presence, they should immediately leave before something happens to them, and notify an adult as fast as possible.

Now let's talk a little about why we should keep all guns locked up in a safe, and why the parents should be the only ones who know the combination. Over the last few years there have been a number of shootings taking place involving troubled youth killing innocent teens at schools. By abiding by this simple rule you might keep a troubled youth from using your weapons in such an atrocity.

Now for the gun control enthusiasts who want to ban guns, I am talking to you from a law enforcement point a view. Banning guns is not the answer. People have the right to bear arms and protect themselves from the criminal element. I have watched the president on TV getting on his phony soapbox screaming for more gun controls laws, but in the same picture he is surrounded by 20 men caring handguns.

No, gun control will not solve a thing. The criminal mind does not abide by laws; as a matter of fact they do not buy guns legally, they buy them on the black market. Most of the fully automatic weapons are being smuggled into the United States to sell to this criminal element. Gun control will only disarm the good citizens, leaving the criminal element in full control.

There is something I learned a long time ago about an unstable mind. Once they decide they are going to do something, no matter what their motive is, they are going to do it. If they do not have a gun to carry out their plan, then they will use a knife. If they are intending on hurting a number of people and they do not have a gun, then they will revert to a bomb. You do not want an unstable youth using a bomb. The casualty rate will be much higher.

It is unfortunate that we have unstable people hell bent on doing harm to innocent people. Usually this occurs for no other reason than just to make a statement; to make people suffer because the individual is suffering themselves. The best way to stop these events from occurring is for parents to open their eyes up at home and identify the fact that they may have an unstable teen who is displaying behavior traits that are not normal.

If a parent becomes alerted to the fact their child is displaying unusual behavior, it may be time to seek out professional help. There is no shame in doing so. The shame will come if your child hurts other people and you did not seek out help for them before it happened. We all need to become a part of the remedy and not the problem.

# CHAPTER 12
## RACISM

Racism is as old as the bible. It has affected ethnic groups in every country in the world in one manner or another. Some countries have evolved past it and some base their social structure on it.

Racism has cost the lives of many people around the world. It has caused countries to hate each other. It has turned ethnic groups within a population against each other due to one suppressing the other. It has caused the slaughter of countless lives and the attempted genocide of complete ethnic groups in more than one country.

The United States was not much different than any other country in the past, which had to evolve through its racist past. In the 1950s and 1960s we had many trying moments in a country made up of many cultures. People were in the streets protesting one group or another. Integration of ethnic groups was taking place in the school systems causing turmoil amongst the ethnic groups and the youth. Adults were pouring to the streets with looks of hate in their eyes.

Then the 1970s came into the picture, and the sense of peace and love was filling the air. As time went on, the protesting stopped and our youth became the building block to suppress racism. They showed the adults the way to get past it by befriending those from other cultures. By doing so they showed the adults of this country that color did not make a person, rather what was inside was what really mattered. As time went on all cultures in the United States eventually emerged together. We accomplished a feat that many countries have not been able to pull off for hundreds of years.

In my opinion racism has been all but wiped out in the United States. There are still racists in the United States and there are those people who claim racism to cover their own downfalls. Is racism wiped out completely? No, and I do not think it will ever be completely wiped out. There are still groups out there such as the Ku Klux Klan and disruptive groups like the Skinheads who will carry their racist sword to the grave.

Racism itself comes in many forms and colors. But racism today is nothing like it was in America earlier in history. Some people say we have just become blind to it. I say that is hogwash; it is not as prominent and out in the open as it was years earlier.

I attribute the success we have had up to this point to the youth of this country, accepting each other no matter what color their skin. Kids today interact as though racism never occurred within this country. They laugh together, they play together, and they take up for each other if an outsider tries to harm one of them. Interracial marriage has become acceptable between different cultures. Yes, the United States has evolved and moved on past the racism of the '50s and '60s.

There are those who utilize the words suppression and racism as nothing more than a crutch to cover up their failure in life. They use it as a means to cover their lazy ways and lack of willingness to succeed.

I applaud people like Bill Cosby, who are constantly trying to reach out to the youth of this country, expressing that we are all in control of our own destiny. He is a man who feels racism has become nothing more than a poor excuse for not succeeding in life and for some a reason not to try. He is a man who is tired of seeing adults lead their youth down a bad road, by giving them crutches and vices to prop themselves up with when they fail.

I wish there were more people out there like him, willing to go against those who want the word racism to stay alive. People who were willing to tell the youth of this country to quit looking for reason to fail, and start looking for ways to succeed. Unfortunately there are people out there who do not want to see racism go away. These people have based their whole lives supposedly on fighting racism and for other peoples' rights. The part you must understand is their livelihood is also based on its existence and they do not want to lose the profits they make off the word racism.

If you live in a poor neighborhood and you are tired of being surrounded by those who have quit trying to succeed, then start looking for a way to get out of that neighborhood. Go to school, whether it is a tech school or college. Make something out of yourself, get a trade that you can support your family. Hard work and sacrifice go a long way to making you a better person who will have much to offer society.

A person who says "I can't" will never succeed. A person who says "I will try" has very little confidence. But a person who says "I will" is already a success without doing anything. Get rid of all the crutches and go after success. It does not matter what color your skin is. Success is at every person's fingertips, it's just a matter of stepping forward to grab it.

Parents, push your children to succeed in life. Do not allow them to have crutches to use as excuses. Ask them what they would like to be when they grow. It will change many time between being a youth and adulthood. But inspire them to believe they can be whatever they want to be in life. Inspiration is probably the most important gift you can give your child. It gives them a sense of direction, and the feeling of not being lost. It makes them believe in you, because you believe in them. And in the end they will know you will be there to support them.

Give them reachable goals, while reinforcing they can be anything they want to be in life. When a child feels their parent believes in them, they feel invincible. Encourage your child to go to college. Let them know the sky is the limit, and you are there to back them 100%.

Established goals are very good for building confidence in their ability to succeed. Some parents say I cannot afford to send my child to college. That may be true, but there are many other ways for a young adult to go to college, if that is what they want to do. Federal student loans are out there for all young adults.

When I am around young adults, I try to make it a point to ask them what direction in life they heading. When they have a blank look on their face, I ask them what they are interested in, and once I get enough information out of them, I try to open doors of possibility. Most kids just need a little guidance to show them the possibility of bringing their dream to life is at their fingertips.

Most young adults who are caught up in a rut and not succeeding in life never received guidance from their parents. They were stuck with no answers on how to go forward with their dreams. Kids who have no idea what direction to take in life are not much different than a car stuck in the mud. Sometimes all they need is just a little encouragement and a stranger to pull them out of the rut they are in to get them moving forward again.

Parents, be a guiding force in your child's life. Do not let vices like the term racism hold your child back. You as a parent should want more for your child than you had. Push them to achieve their goals in life. Do not let outside people influence their lives by giving them excuses to fall back on if they at first do not succeed.

# CHAPTER 13
## MENTAL HEALTH
## SYSTEM/REHABILITATION

A U.S. survey of adolescents in 2010, published in the *Archives of General Psychiatry,* indicates that one in every five youths aged 13 to 18 in the United States is likely to have experienced a mental disorder with severe impairment at some point. The survey also stated that 8% of U.S. teens experienced serious emotional disturbances, and just over 40% experienced some sort of mental disorder. Mental illness, whether a person was born with it or it became a learned trait that just got out of hand, surrounds us every day in our normal lives. The old expression, "Just take time and smell the coffee," comes into play here. If you would just slow down and take the time to watch your environment, you will see traces of mental illness in some of the people you come in contact with every day.

There are so many people who refuse to recognize the fact that another person does not act right. Most people would identify them as being just different. What they should be saying is that person is not all there and they need some professional help.

As a parent it is your job to control your child's environment until they are capable of making good decisions. In an earlier chapter we talked about the impact violent movies and games have on our children's mental status. We need to also recognize some of the things that have a mind changing impact on our children, such as divorce, the death of a parent and those things a child considers being failures in life.

These simple things can take a normal child and turn their world completely upside down quickly, leaving them full of hate, anger and very little hope. You take such a dramatic impact on a child delicate world, add all the violence they have been watching on TV, in conjunction with the video games, and you could find yourself with a time bomb waiting to go off.

The first step to identifying mental illness in another person is to take off the blinders and be willing to recognize it. The next thing is to get that person some professional help. So many of us just do not want to be bothered with other peoples' problems. We walk through life always looking the other way.

Society has become more and more filled with individuals showing signs of mental illness. Due to it becoming more prevalent, the chances are great that you will be impacted at some point in your life by someone who is mentally imbalanced, whether it is a violent ex-husband, or a mentally disturbed person who is strung out on drugs.

The ages of people showing mental illness signs range from children to adults, from the kid attending your child's school to the bum walking down the street talking to themselves. It is so important for you to know your environment. It is also important to know who your children hang out with when you are not around.

When you are in the presence of kids showing signs of depression or mental illness such as violent outbursts, do not be afraid to ask other adults if they are being treated for their symptoms. Too many adults look the other way these days. Parents in general should bring it to the school's attention, and find out if they know about this child and if something is being done to assist them.

If something is not done to help this child things are going to just get worse for them. It is tough for a child who has emotional problems. They do not know what is wrong with them. They figure out at some point they are different than the rest of their peers, but do not know how to fix it. They are more than likely embarrassed about their condition and may not know who to turn to for help.

While coaching sports in high school, I have come across so many kids who could not handle defeat or being outdone by another player while in practice. They would get so mentally clouded in their heads, they would start talking to themselves, asking out loud in front of all the other kids, "What's wrong with me, why can't I get it right?" This is usually followed up by an physical outburst, such as striking themselves to the head area with their hand, while throwing their equipment to the ground as hard as they can.

There have been many times I have had to pull an athlete out of practice to calm them down. When talking with someone who is emotionally unstable, you have to maintain a low, calm tone of voice, to bring their temperament down to a normal level. You basically have to talk to them as though they were a young child, assuring them that everything will be alright, while enforcing that their outburst was distracting and unproductive for that environment.

Over the years I have seen this type of mental meltdown many times in people from young children on the streets to adults in the prison system. When they get to this point, you can see in their eyes that no one is at home at that particular moment. They look through you like you are not there and they are not hearing a word you are saying. You must always remember to communicate to a person in this mental state with a low tone of voice and not take on an aggressive mannerism, because if you do, you may be perceived as a threat to them, and find yourself being assaulted.

The only thing that works with kids going through an abnormal emotional state is to pull them out of the situation for a while and to allow them to regroup their mental status. This has to be done to ensure they do not hurt themselves, or more importantly someone else.

These type of kids a lot of times are very nice and pleasant to be around, but when they are put under a stress load the other side of them comes out. A lot of times they go untreated for their problems because their mom and dad think it is just a behavior issue or a shame to bring it to the professional's attention.

I want you to understand something. There is nothing normal about a child or adult who talks to themselves while repeatedly striking themselves to the head area, nor is it normal for them to beat their heads against the wall. All this amounts to is one thing; they are punishing themselves by inflicting pain for their failures. This is showing an act of aggression and uncontrollable rage in conjunction with a lack of reasoning.

Such an outburst is not unlike behavior exhibited by a self mutilator. When they reach their breaking point they act out by hurting themselves because they see themselves as being a failure, or they want attention.

I once asked an inmate who was a self mutilator why he did it. He answered by saying it was a way to cleanse himself of his failures. Whether it is a way to rectify failure, get attention or get even with someone else, these are all signs of danger and will progressively get worse as time goes on. If you notice these signs being portrayed by your child, get them help by a professional. Do not let your own pride stand in the way. Get the child some counseling for his/her sake and those around them.

I once knew a kid at my son's high school who had severe emotional issues. While playing sports he could not accept defeat. When he lost a wrestling match he immediately would go into a violent rage, throwing his equipment, stomping off the floor and engulfing himself in a hate-filled outburst.

I often wondered if this child ever received counseling from a professional, but his issues were never rectified and brought under control. He eventually joined the military after high school. Within a year and a half of being in the military, he came home on leave and hung himself in a public place for all to see.

This young adult had made it a point to ensure everyone knew when he was upset, and I cannot keep from thinking he hung himself in public because he wanted everyone to witness he was unhappy about his life.

If your child is emotionally unstable, the last place they belong is in the military. The military makes an immature person grow up by giving them stability, by making them accountable for themselves, but they're not in the business of correcting mental illness. If anything it produces mental illness in a lot of servicemen because of the war atmosphere they may be thrown into.

Homeless people are very volatile individuals. Most of them have damaged their mental status by utilizing drugs and abusing alcohol. They have given up on society and they have given up on themselves. The harsh environment they live in on a daily basis, accompanied with the tremendous lack of nourishment, food, vitamins etc., takes toll on their well-being. All this in conjunction with living in the harsh elements of the freezing cold weather in the winter and the overwhelming heat in the summer, causes their mental health status to quickly deteriorate.

These same traits were found in POWs from past wars. POWs who were starved and mistreated by their captors, became very mentally deranged, taking on the fight or flight complex along with the mental status of survival of the fittest.

When you come in contact with a mentally ill person living on the streets, you do not know if they are going to perceive you as a threat or someone they can easily prey on. You do not know if you are in the company of Dr. Jekyll or Mr. Hyde. You must be careful with these types of people, especially if you are a woman or a child.

People showing traits of mental illness are walking time bombs and very unstable individuals who could snap at any moment. We have seen this over the years with teenagers going into their schools, and killing their classmates. All of the perpetrators involved in these school shootings had one thing in common; "They were suffering from some type of mental illness."

Some of them had withdrawn themselves from society. They took on the "It's me against the world" attitude. They narrowed their list of friends down to one or two, who had a similar mindset or interest. These types of kids start feeding off of each other and can take each other's mental status downhill fast. For whatever reason these kids get to the point of taking another human life, and it all started with some type of sign that was ignored by other adults.

The signs could be as simple as a violent outburst toward other family members or those they come into contact with, withdrawing themselves from those who are very close to them, hiding out in their room and never coming out, all while being totally sucked up into the secure world they have created for themselves. These are simple signs that something is wrong, and you as a parent need to intervene.

There are many cults or trends forming in the teenage society. They are constantly looking for new kids to recruit to join in their suffering. What is a cult? A cult is a group or organization that bases its existence on a specific belief system, which results in unhealthy obsessions and compulsions.

They are a tight-knit group who worry about outsiders that may tell other people about what they stand for and what they are up to. They have no respect for what other people think if it is not in line with what they believe in. They are constantly looking for other kids to prey on. Kids who are lost and confused usually become easy targets. Cults tend to brainwash their members from the reality of society, offer them everything that is considered wrong in mainstream society, all while isolating them from the rest of the world.

For a child confused about life, a cult will begin as a way to escape the world. They will step up, begin giving a confused child the answer to that which has put them into conflict. The survival of a cult is based on how good they are at deception. In the end the goal of a cult is to take over the teen's life and emotional status. This type of cult is considered an organized cult.

There are other cults that may be less organized, such as Goths, that have a negative impact on a child's emotional state. The Gothic moment leaves a child in the reality state that they are nothing more than the walking dead. They take on the attitude, "It is no use to try, I am dead, I do not need anyone to acknowledge my existence and there is nothing out there for me." They dress in pure black, and put black makeup around their eyes to symbolize darkness and death.

Cult type groups can have a very negative impact on a child's mindset, a lasting impact that might stay with them for the rest of their lives even after they leave the group. We are all looking for something to believe in. It is human nature to be like this. The big thing as a parent is you need to know what element or groups your children are connecting themselves with.

Look at Jim Jones and the Guyana tragedy. Jones was a Communist Party member who formed a non-denominational religious group known as The Peoples Temple, eventually moving his church from Indiana to the Redwood Valley, California area. When Jones was born his mother proclaimed she had given birth to the messiah and repeatedly proclaimed this to Jones. Jones was raised to believe he was a very special messenger, who was sent from God. His father was said to be a member of the order of the Ku Klux Klan.

Jones later claimed to be the messiah, the reincarnation of Jesus, to his followers. His congregation grew fast, while he drugged his members with the opiate of religion. He eventually moved his flock to Guyana to get away from government restrictions and influences. Once there, Jones took on more and more the role of being Jesus with his members, and started taking liberties with members' wives.

Eventually members attempted to leave the colony because Jones' teachings had grown so far-fetched, they had lost faith in him. Members of the cult attempting to leave were not allowed to go. Word eventually got back to Congress in Washington that members were being held against their will, resulting in Congressman Leo Ryan and his staff going to Guyana to investigate the issue. The end result was they were assassinated prior to them leaving Guyana. After the assassination Jones knew there would be a huge price to pay for the assassination of Ryan. Jones then ordered the "mass suicide" or murders of his colony to be carried out.

As a parent, it is very important you know the element your children are socializing with. You need to help your child form sensible goals and assist them in finding reasonable things to believe in, because those surrounding them in society can be misleading as Jim Jones was.

Parents with children born with mental illness have all my respect. This is a very difficult situation. I truly feel for parents raising a mentally ill child a child who loves you one moment and the next has a knife in their hand threatening to kill you. This type of parent should be awarded a medal for bravery for the torment their nerves go through on a daily basis.

The undying love and devotion they have for their child; the sleepless nights after each outburst over the simplest thing as asking them to brush their teeth; the endless days they go through wondering what will happen to their child should they die. Then they have to constantly worry about how much more aggressive their child is getting as they grow in age and the worry and hope that their child does not hurt someone outside of the family. They lay in wait, hoping medical research will present a cure for the illness their child possesses, or at least a new drug that will bring their child under control and back to some type of normalcy.

# CHAPTER 14
## TEENAGE SEX

What a very controversial subject. Depending on who you talk to, you will get a wide variety of opinions. Let's throw out all the religious points of view, because we already know where religion stands on sex before marriage, and how the church does not approve of it. Let's just get down to the common sense of what can happen if two teenagers start experimenting with sex, and how such a pleasurable act, as innocent as it seems, can destroy their promising lives quickly.

Peer pressure today on teenage kids is unbelievable when it comes to sex. Most people think about the pressure on girls to have sex, but we are going to start out with the young boys in this case. Boys are not as advanced as girls in age versus maturity. In my opinion it seems boys are about two years behind young girls. When girls get to a certain age they are trying to attract the eyes of a boy, while the boys are still running around playing tag with each other.

Boys start losing that "girls are yucky" attitude at about 12. At this age, they are not really interested in them, but they are starting to notice little things about girls who are around them. They may even have a part-time girlfriend, who they hang out with. At this age holding hands is a really big deal.

By the time they reach 14 most boys are venturing out looking to find their first girlfriend. And for most boys this is when they get introduced to a whole lot of lies from their male counterparts, who conjure up the most unbelievable stories about what they have experienced with girls. As we all know 99.1% of these stories are only a figment of their imagination. This is the age group that starts feeling the peer pressure to live up to their friends' expectations. Girls are much more advanced at this age. They are definitely looking for their version of romance. They start wearing tighter clothes, showing off their bodies. They are not necessarily looking for sexual encounter, but rather more holding, talking, understanding and their first knight in shining armor.

By the time a boy hits 15 his hormones are going crazy, and he is now noticing everything. When he is in the company of a beautiful girl, his heart starts pounding hard, and if they happen to talk to him for the first time, his face turns blood red. Girls on the other hand are much more outgoing at this age, very much a free spirit.

By the time a boy hits 16, sexual encounter is right at his door step. The peer pressure is unbearable. Sex talk is all around them, even if it is just sexual related jokes. When in the company of friends it is not unusual for them to be ask point blank, "Have you had sex with your girlfriend yet?"

They will make up the most ridiculous story to cover up whether or not sex has actually occurred. If they were taught right at home, there is only one answer, "It is none of your business." That way no one gets hurts behind a ridiculous conversation.

Immature minds do not always put together the right answers to tough questions. They seem to always forget whose company they are in. If they tell them they have had sex with their young lady friend, it will be all over the school by the end of the day.

This creates a tough situation, more so for the young lady. The young boy is looked upon by the guys as being a lucky stud, and by a lot of the other young girls as a desirable future target for them because he is considered to be experienced. But unfortunately for the young lady, whether it is true or not, her name will be spread around the school and the social network as being easy or even by a crueler word utilized by girls when talking bad about another, "She's a whore."

You as a parent need to sit down with your young lady entering into the high school shark tank. Teach her to have a game plan, a set of rules by which future boyfriends must follow to be a part of her life. They must go in knowing young boys are pressured by friends to give all the juicy details about their girlfriends.

They must have an understanding with the new boyfriend that he is to never talk about her in a less than gentlemanly manner to his friends. And if he is being pressured to give answers about their sexual encounters, then the answer is simple "It is none of your business." If he cannot abide by this simple rule then he is not worth having around.

Kids today are much more advanced when it comes to sex. When I was 14 looking at a *Playboy* magazine was a big deal. It was a big secret you kept from your parents, so you could continue to do it. These day's kids see what amounts to nothing more than soft porn all day long on TV. They even have animated cartoons which show graphic sex scenes.

Sex education is now being taught to children at age 14, and the ways things are going it probably will be offered at the elementary level sooner or later. No one is untouched by peer pressure, not even preacher's daughters or sons. They are just as bad or worse when it comes to sex and in some cases alcohol.

I think preachers' kids use their status as a way to blind their parents to what they are up to when they are not around them, and in some cases to get even for having religion pushed on them so hard. I once had a preacher friend who was quite wild as a teen. He had pulled up to a stop sign with his vehicle and had his arm around his girlfriend. In the lane next to him, a police officer pulled up beside him. Seeing he had only one hand on the steering wheel, he yelled out of his window, "Use both hands." My preacher friend looked back at the officer and stated, "If I use both hands how will I drive?"

I was a preacher's son. my step dad was a preacher and a very knowledgeable man when it came to the bible. But I will tell you I was no different than any other kids out there. I checked the girls out, I had girlfriends like any other teenager, and we did things that we were lucky did not get us in trouble.

Is sex education the answer? Well, I cannot say it hurts. But this definitely opens up doors for acceptance amongst teenagers. In some aspects it sends a message that we cannot stop you, so we want you to be safe while you are experimenting. I would not be so hard on this subject if everything always turned out great, but most of the time this is not the case. The young girl comes up pregnant, the boy gets scared and the next thing she knows, her knight in shining armor turned out to be nothing more than a careless frog who disappeared from her life in the middle of the night.

Now I think the answer to this problem starts at home. In today's society I believe there is a lack of respect for the opposite sex and another person's feelings. When you are raised by a parent who thinks having a positive conversation with their son is asking "Did you get any yet?" then I believe we need to go back to the drawing board.

Now guys be honest, in your life have you ever asked your son or another friend that question? Parents need to ensure their kids are taught to respect the opposite sex and their feelings. When it is time to have sex it will just happen. It is not an action that should be conducted under pressure by the opposite sex. You should not feel that if you do not give in, you will lose your boyfriend or girlfriend.

If we start stepping up at home and instill good morals into our kids, morals that say treat a woman like a lady, morals in young girls that indicates do not give in to peer pressure, then maybe we can start making some headway in regards to teen pregnancy.

Girls need to be taught to demand they be treated like a lady. They should understand if a boy is pressuring them to have sex, then maybe he is not the right person for them. If the young man cares about them, he will wait until the time is right.

When I was growing up I was taught to treat a woman like a lady. I have tried to practice that trait my whole life. I feel a lot of children are not receiving this type of training at home. If boys are taught to respect girls as being young ladies, and conduct themselves as gentlemen in their company, maybe we would not have a need for sex education.

The number one thing a teenager better take into consideration before having sex is, is this Mr. or Mrs. Right, because one slip up and they just became that person. Teenage peer pressure in regards to sex is a rough issue. But, if we as parents start attacking this issue at home, maybe we can relieve some of this pressure on future teenagers.

The United States has the highest teen pregnancy rate in the Western world. Teen pregnancy was considered higher prior to 1980 than it is now. This was due to teen marriages being more acceptable at that time.

Most of today's teen pregnancies occur outside of marriage. The following are statistics gathered by Teen Help. Even though the teen pregnancy rate has declined, the United States still averages 820,000 non-wed teen pregnancies a year. This results in 34% of teens being pregnant before they reach 20. 79% of those teen girls are not married and 80% are by accident.

Statistics show four in ten teenage girls have intercourse at the age of 13 and fourteen. The highest rate of teen pregnancy is amongst teen girls who are 15 and under.

Teen pregnancy can really ruin a young girl or young man's life. It is said that only 1/3 of teen mothers who get pregnant finish high school. Because their life was turned upside down at the flip of a switch, only 1.5% go on to college. Teen Help indicates 80% of pregnant unmarried teen girls end up on welfare. Teen Help gathered the following information from teens themselves:

- 82% feel that teens should not be sexually active.
- 72% agreed that teens who are sexually active should have access to birth control.

73% feel that being a <u>virgin</u> should not be embarrassing.

- 58% feel that high school age teens should not be sexually active, and fewer than half of teens in high school have had sex.
- 67% of teens who have had sex wish that they had waited (60 percent of boys and 77 percent of girls).

It is important you start talking to your teens about sex. Outline the life-changing event of getting pregnant or getting someone pregnant. Talk to them about the diseases that are sexually transmitted, some of which they will never recover from.

Now let's briefly talk about another tough subject; young adults living together or what we use to call "shacking up" before marriage. I know as far as a religion goes, it is not acceptable, and I to was raised in religion. But if I was asked what I felt about it, I would say this: young adults of proper age should live together for at least six months before they enter into marriage.

I am expressing this because there has been a long running trend of new marriages falling apart within the first year. You can date each other for years, but you really do not get to know each other until you live under the same roof. When you exist in two separate houses, you can get away from each other if you need your space. You also do not see those annoying habits your lover possesses until you move in together.

It is far better to live together for a few months before marriage. This gives you the ability to figure out if you can stand the other person's bad morning personality or bad habits for the rest of your life. This is better learned before getting married, rather than learning it after you are newly married, resulting in fighting and divorce.

According to statistics, married adults now divorce two-and-a-half times as often as adults did 20 years ago and four times as often as they did 50 years ago. 50% of new marriages will eventually end in divorce. The probability within the first five years is 20%, and the probability of its ending within the first 10 years is 33%. Statistics say 25% of children ages 16 and under live with a stepparent. Surveys also indicate the annual divorce rate is half of the annual marriage rate in most states.

Now let us discuss rape, or date rape. As parents we must make our young ladies aware there are a lot of people out there who might target them for sex. In regards to rape by a stranger we will keep it simple. It is our duty to teach our young ladies to always be aware of their environment.

They should not place themselves in a situation where they can be caught all alone out of the public eye when not at home, walking down dark alleys, being out in the streets at night alone, finding themselves alone with a perfect stranger and the list goes on.

Teach them that the world is less than perfect. Make them aware if they always think about being cautious, it will go a long way to ensuring they do not get harmed in any way. Teens feel invincible and all they think about is having fun. Unfortunately they do not think about the bad things that can happen to them when not at home.

Date rape is a more prominent form of rape. It can happen by a boyfriend or teens who are considered very good acquaintances. Our young ladies need to know if they attend a school function such as a dance or prom, they need to be aware of what can happen to ruin their night.

We need to make them aware of drugs utilized in the party scene to make a young lady pass out such as Rohypnol, which also goes by street names like circles, mind eraser, roach and GHB. Teach our children not to take pills to be a part of the in crowd and to be very careful who they accept drinks that could be laced with a narcotic.

Make them understand being around boys and drinking large amounts of alcohol can lead to date rape, especially if the young man has less than honorable morals. He may be a repeat offender of date rape or just a young man wanting sex and thinking she is passed out, she will never know. A lot of times the young lady says nothing about it and carries it around inside her for a very long time, before they open up, telling someone else about what happened.

We need to teach our young men to be better than this. They need to understand it is not right to demoralize another person by taking advantage of them when they are vulnerable. They need to understand drugging someone, or having sex with another person without their consent, is illegal and called rape. Such a simple act can land them in prison for a very long time.

Our teens also need to be taught to take care of someone who is under the influence to the point another person might take advantage of them, even if they do not like them. They need to be taught to get them out of the environment and get them home safely.

# CHAPTER 15
## DRUG ADDITION

Parents today are faced with one of the most difficult battles in today's society. The battle is called raising a drug free child. Communication between the parent and child is one of the most powerful tools we have at our disposal. Addressing the dangers of drug use will assist you in keeping your child drug free.

Unfortunately there are a lot of parents who do not take the time to talk to their children about the health risk drugs pose. Some parents believe their child will not partake in drug use. Other parents simply do not think about addressing the issue.

Peer pressure is a very strong issue when it comes to drugs. If you do not do what everyone else is doing then you are not a part of the in crowd. It seems the discussion with children about drug addiction and how badly it will ruin their life does not happen as much as it should. We must talk to our children on a continuing basis about the dangers of drug use, and continue to be active participants in their lives on this issue.

Drugs are only good for one thing, and that one thing is ruining young people's lives. I consider drug dealers as being parasites. They make money off of our youth by sucking the last bit of life they have out of them.

Drugs and alcohol are the number one thing you as a parent have to worry about. No matter how good a parent you are, or how hard you try to keep your child from drugs and alcohol, they will come in contact with them sooner or later. You as a parent can only hope your child will fall back on the words of advice you gave them about drug use. They must be taught to withstand peer pressure, and the temptation to try drugs "just once," because their friends insist they are not cool if they do not.

Inform your children not to be tempted to smoke cigarettes with their friends. A lot of drug addicts will lace their cigarettes so they can have their drugs at school undetected. The simplest thing as trying to be cool and smoke a harmless cigarette with friends can cause a lifetime of problems. I know. I had a child that smoked a innocent cigarette at school that turned out to be laced, and that cigarette led to years of hardship and sleepless

nights for her, my wife and I.

Teen Drug Abuse reported statistics indicating 40% of those who started drinking at age 13 or younger developed alcohol dependence later in life. Ten percent of teens that began drinking after the age of 17 developed dependence. Teens that drink are 50 times more likely to use cocaine than teens who never consumed alcohol. Sixty-three percent of the youth who drink alcohol say that they initially got the alcohol from their home or their friend's homes. Alcohol kills 6½ times more teenagers than all other illicit drugs combined. More than 60% of teens said drugs were sold, used, or kept at their school. Twenty percent of 8th graders report that they have tried marijuana. Twenty-eight percent of teens know a classmate or friend who has used ecstasy.

Peer pressure is a very tough situation for a teen. Every child wants to have friends and fit in with a social group their age. You as a parent hope you have taught them well enough to be able to say "no" and mean it. Ten percent of teens report they have attended raves parties where ecstasy and other drugs were available.

Studies indicate approximately 15% of 10th through 12th graders have used amphetamines. In a study at San Francisco General Hospital, 25% of the seizures in youth patients were found to be caused by amphetamine use. NIDA indicates use of cocaine is up amongst students at the 10 grades level from 1.0% to 1.8% and 12 grade level from 2.6% to 4.6% .

I raised around drugs. I was taught to stay away from drug use by my older brother, who was using drugs at the time. Even though he was always under the influence, he would tell me when we were alone together, should he ever catch me taking any narcotics, he would beat me within a inch of my life. He was being very sincere. He did not want me to go through the addiction and the emotions that he was faced with each day of his life.

Your only tool as a parent to ward off drug use is to constantly talk to your children about how drugs ruin peoples' lives. Teen Drug Abuse reports teenagers whose parents talks to them on a regular basis about the dangers of drug use are 42% less likely to use them than those whose parents do not. Take them for a little tour around town and show them people who failed to listen and fell into the grips of temptation to just try it one time. Show them all the people living under the bridge in town; the people who allowed drugs and alcohol to consume their lives to the point they lost everything they had to include their personal identity.

Inform them about the various drugs out there on the streets. Take time to learn a little bit about drugs yourself so you know what you're talking about. Let your child know that there are many drugs which can be addictive even if they are only used once.. Drugs such as cocaine are called the rich man's drug because it is a one-time use addiction and the high is only five minutes, leaving the user wanting more.

The drugs of choice today for teenagers and young adults are marijuana and methamphetamine (meth). Methamphetamine is the drug of choice because it is cheap to purchase and readily available. Meth is very dangerous because of the chemicals used in the processing. Chemicals such as Drano, acid and red phosphorous, which are all poisonous , resulting in massive sores on the body.

Meth acts a lot like speed. Watch your child for staying up all night with endless energy. A person on meth can stay awake for three days without sleep. They cannot sit still. They want to constantly be doing something. After being strung out on meth for a long period of time, hallucinations start kicking in from sleep deprivation. They will hallucinate about things such as someone trying to break in through their bedroom window in the middle of the night, to having spiders crawling on them. In the end, I am not sure that the meth actually kills the user, but rather the lack of sleep, which weakens the heart to a state of failure.

For those of you who have children addicted to drugs, I feel bad for you. As a parent I have been there. I want you to know drug addiction touches people from all walks of life, from children of doctors, lawyers, and NFL coaches to people in law enforcement. I want you to know you're not alone. There are many parents just like you dealing with a child who is addicted to drugs.

As a parent with a child who is an addict, it is normal to feel guilt and a sense of failure. If you as a parent have done all you can to educate your child about the repercussions of using drugs, then you need to snap out of this emotional state you're in. The sooner you come to grips with yourself, the sooner you can put a plan into effect to help your child to recovery.

The best advice I can give you is find out where your child is getting their drug supply. Turn each one of their drug suppliers in to the police, eliminating each supplier one at a time. You must always reinforce the fact that you are there for your child, no matter how hard it is on you, because in the end your love for them is what gets them through the addiction state to the recovery road.

Never give up on your child. You're all they have to lean on, and your persistence and support is all they have. In most cases they have already given up on themselves, but they lean on you as a crutch because they know you love them, and you have faith that they will eventually find the courage and strength to fight their drug addiction.

I have spent many sleepless nights wondering where my addicted teen was after she had snuck out of her bedroom window in the middle of the night. Each time we would go looking for her and eventually bring her home. Each time it was a struggle and a fight, with many unpleasant words exchanged. But because we went after her and because we reinforced that we cared, she eventually found the strength to walk away from drug addiction, which had taken her hostage.

If your child runs away, go find them. You will not be able to sleep while your mind is wondering where they are and if they are safe. Each time you find them, bring them home, no matter how much they resist you. It reassures them how much you care. A person on drugs can say terrible things to those who love them most. Just remember it is the drugs talking and not the person who you love so much.

A person addicted to drugs has an inner demon who tries to control their every emotion a demon who lashes out at you when you threaten their existence and get in the way of them finding their next fix. Drugs can be beat, but the person who is addicted has to hit rock bottom before you can help them.

If you take a person to a drug rehab clinic who has not hit rock bottom yet, or is not willing to follow your advice, you are wasting your money. I have seen it over and over again, parents and family members spending a lot of money to get one of their love ones sobered up, just to have them go out and get a fix. You only hope they hit rock bottom before the drugs kill them.

Only the addicted person can determine when they are ready to fight their addiction. People with drug addiction hate themselves for what they have become. What you as a parent have to watch out for is your child coming in contact with close friends or family members who are addicts. I always say misery loves company. Addicts will go out and find people close to them to join them in their addiction so they have someone else doing wrong just as bad as they are.

Like I said it is important for you to show your addicted child you care and assure them you love them, even if it is tough love. Nothing you do or say goes unnoticed, and hopefully they will get to the point that they no longer like the person they see in the mirror.

Now I want you to be aware that when an addict hits the rock bottom stage, they are in a fragile state of mind. They call this hitting rock bottom because the addicted person has given up on themselves and hates what they have become. When a lot of addicts hit this point, they are very confused and emotionally unbalanced, and contemplate suicide to end their pain. Their inner demon is telling them they are weak and they cannot fight their drug addiction. Hopefully they will reach out to you at this point. At this time your support factor must be at its strongest.

It has been reported by National Institute of Justices Arrestee and Drug Monitoring System (ADAM) that most teens that are arrested often test positive for recent drug use and 66% of underage male arrestees tested positive for marijuana.

There has been a modest reporting that illicit drug use has gone down a bit since the 1970s. It is being reported that this is due to how teens are starting to perceive the dangers of using drugs. Although the use of some drugs has gone down, the National Institute for Drugs has reported statistics from 2012 indicating the use of marijuana amongst teens is on the rise.

# CHAPTER 16
## GANGS/ DISRUPTIVE GROUPS

Gangs and disruptive groups are made up of people with the same mindset, in which they work together to conduct illicit, law breaking activity in the name of the group. These groups prey on our children and eat away at their soul and moral fiber. In the end, this leaves them broken, empty and ruined.

There are three main situations which lead to a teen being influenced to become a gang member. The first type is a teen who is following in their family's footsteps. The next is a teen who lives in a neighborhood which has been overrun by a particular gang. And the last is a teen who befriends a gang member, resulting in them being introduced to the gang lifestyle.

The Federal Bureau of Investigation indicates there are approximately 1.4 million active street, prison, and Outlaw Motorcycle Group gang members in the United States. They also indicate there are approximately 33,000 identified gangs throughout the nation. The West Coast and Great Lakes regions have the most identified gangs, but membership has been on the rise in Northeast and Southeast regions of the nation.

It appears the disruptive gangs such as Southern Hispanic "Surenos" are expanding their territory nationally. It is also noted that ethnic-based gangs are increasing in number, such as African, Asian, Caribbean, and Euro gangs.

Gangs are responsible for an average of 48% of violent crimes which occur in the nation. In the major cities and suburban areas gang violence has been on the rise. The neighborhood-based gangs and drug crews are still the most significant criminal threat to our community. Gangs are aggressively recruiting new juvenile members and expanding their territory.

The Federal Bureau of Investigation indicates many jurisdictions are experiencing an increase in juvenile gang violence, which is often attributed to increased incarceration rates of older members and the aggressive recruitment of juveniles in schools.

Gangs target youths because of their vulnerability and susceptibility to recruitment tactics, as well as their likelihood to not receive harsh criminal sentencing early on.

Juvenile gang members in some communities are hosting parties and organizing special events which develop into opportunities for recruiting, drug use, sexual exploitation, and criminal activity.

Gangster Rap gangs, often comprised of juveniles, are forming and are being used to launder drug money through seemingly legitimate businesses, according to National Gang Intelligence Center reporting.

What do gangs have to offer a teen? Just about anything a parent will say no to. Most gangs offer a false sense of brotherhood. Gang members live life in the fast lane, which is appealing to young kids. They usually end up dropping out of school and receive their education on the streets.

Gangs prey on confused teens who are looking for something to believe in by flashing money, painting a picture of a more exciting lifestyle, late night parties, women, drugs, alcohol, and avenues to make some fast money illegally.

Gangs stand for every negative quality you can imagine. They suck teens in under a false sense of security, while using and abusing them, after which they become expendable. Their personal makeup is totally the opposite of what you want your child to turn out like. If allowed they will suck your teen in by befriending them, while picking the right moment to counteract your wishes by giving your teen something you said no to, such as a vehicle to borrow. Whatever the bait is, once they accept it they will owe the gang a debt.

This seems to be a standard move for any criminal element. First they befriend you, then they play on your emotions to get you to rack up a debt. Nothing is free when it comes to the criminal element. In due time they will want repayment. The payback they expect will be costly and usually involves breaking the law.

Gangs are not built on morals, although most of them do have a code of conduct, put together to benefit the gang itself and its leadership. They bait new recruits by being kind to them, reinforcing that they would never treat them the way other adults do.

They tell them they will be treated with respect and like men as long as they hang out with them.

They will be respected by everyone as long as they're a member of that particular group.

The only problem with gangs is sooner or later, you as a member will be asked to conduct some type of illegal action in the name of the gang. To become a street gang member, most gang require you to be jumped in. The jump initiation usually consists of a new recruit having to fight two or three members of that particular gang at one time. What it really amounts to is about a 30 to 60 second beat down, to prove you have what it takes to be a member of that particular group.

Once a new member has been initiated, it's not uncommon for them to be taken out to test their courage, while committing their first official act for the gang. This usually comes in the form of a drive-by shooting, a walk-up shooting, or moving large amounts of drugs. No matter what the situation is, it will be high risk a risk the leadership does not want to take themselves.

If it is a drive-by, as soon as it occurs the rival gang will find out who conducted it and put a hit out on that individual. This basically means from that point forward, that individual will be running scared, looking over his shoulder every inch of the way.

Now I do not need to say this, but I will. You as a parent need to know exactly who your children are associating with. If it looks like a bad influence, end it. When you're young teen hits the point in life where he feels lost, you need to be there to guide them through it. If you do not, someone else with bad intentions will, such as gang members.

If you move to a new neighborhood make sure it is not a gang neighborhood. You do not want to place your child into this situation. I have talked to so many gang members over the years, most of whom do not want their children to follow in their footsteps. Once they ruin their lives in the name of the gang and waste most of their life behind bars, they start realizing how bad of a mistake they made.

They will usually tell their kids not to get involved in gang activity, but while dad has been away in prison for so long, the local neighborhood gang has already been grooming the young child's mind.

If you are a concerned parent, move your child out of the area, get them out of the element, or start clearing your calendar so you will be able to go visit them in jail or prison. Make sure you enroll your child in activities that will keep all their spare time occupied. Like I said earlier, keeping a child's mind occupied keeps them out of trouble.

Now let's look at some of the various pressure groups which might be a negative influence on your child.

• The Hispanic street gangs are Northern Hispanics and Southern Hispanics which are comprised of many street sets across the nation. These two groups are heavily influenced by the Mexican Mafia and the Nuestra Familia. Their main objective is to make money through drug sales.

• Black disruptive groups are numerous and have strongholds across the nation. I will just mention some of the larger groups such as Bloods and Crips, which are made up of many street sets.

Like most gangs their main objective is to make money.

• Probably one of the largest white disruptive groups is Skinheads, which are made up of many sets. They are Neo Nazi White Supremacist groups whose numbers have grown large across the nation and even in other countries.

Most Skinheads consider themselves to be religion-based, utilizing the ancient Viking Nordic religions. Skinheads are very prejudiced against all other races and do not particularly like other whites if they are not associated with them.

In their mindset, if you are not white then you are an impure race. Skinheads are known for committing hate crimes. They will try to recruit young people into their group by polluting their minds with hate for other races, based on the pure race theory. They will attempt to make their prospects believe their way is the only way and other races are dragging them down.

These are only a few examples of groups whom your child may come in contact with on a daily basis. The bottom line, keep your child's free time occupied. Make it a point to know who they socialize with. Keep their family life secure and happy and they should turn out just fine.

# CHAPTER 17
## POLITICS

Politics and religion are the two subjects associated with starting the most wars around the world. Different political opinions can turn best friends into enemies quickly, and make family members take off the gloves and go to bare knuckles fast.

Politicians are always in the news, pitching their point of view for others to hear, while trying to drum up support for their agenda. They are supposed to be role models for society.

A lot of adults seem to believe our children do not conceive anything about politics, but that is where you are wrong. My six-year-old granddaughter came home from school one day, telling me she was voting for Mitt Romney in the presidential race. My mouth dropped open. I could not believe that a six-year-old took time out from her busy schedule on the monkey bars to contemplate who she was going to vote for, nonetheless know who both candidates for president are.

Kids are very much in tune these days with things going on around them. They hear adults discussing subject matters of all kinds all the time. Sometimes those discussion may be about things they do not need to hear about, so keep that in mind. Nevertheless, they end up sharing what they hear with their playground friends.

Politicians have a very big impact on all of our lives. We hope when we vote for them they will do the right thing and represent us in the manner they said they would. You know, the campaign promises they made to get your vote. Unfortunately more often than not, it does not work out that way.

I once listened to a senator from Alaska, I believe it was retired Senator Gravel (Dem) speaking before the San Jose Bar Association while he was considering running for president in the 2008. During the question and answer period, he was asked how much power does the voter have over a candidate today and how far does that power extend.

Even though I am a registered Republican I admired this man for the honest answers he gave. He was very direct and forthcoming person who pulled no punches while truthfully answering all questions.

He started off by telling the panel he would never win the Democratic nomination, because he was not politically correct within his party's eyes. He went on to answer the question about the power of the voter by saying you as a voter are in full control until you cast your ballet. After that everything the candidate told you to get your vote may go out the door, and his own agenda may kick in.

The United States government from birth was constructed with the idea that the powerful and wealthy would be fully in charge. For the longest period of time, the only way you could be a politician was to be wealthy. Most offices being held were considered a lifetime commitment, or at least until the person holding it gave it up. Then under President Andrew Jackson things began to change. The common man was allowed to vote for the candidate whom he felt was more capable of speaking for the common man.

Today's politicians seem to tell the voters what they want to hear and once elected into office do another thing. It does not matter if they are a Republican or a Democrat, it seems they have their own agenda and sometimes bought and paid for by big business or politically motivated groups.

On April 4th, 2012, a bill was signed to stop congress members from being involved in insider trading. I cannot believe a bill had be put forward to stop such an unlawful thing from happening, especially since we are supposed to be able to trust those we vote into office to make ethical decisions.

It is no secret insider trading has been illegal for years and many people have gone to prison for being involved in such actions. It appears there is going to have to be a bill put forward to stop lobbyists and special interest groups from buying federal and state level politicians as well. It seems the politicians of today are only going into office to get wealthier. All these payoffs from lobbyists and special interest groups are going to have to come to an end to get some true honest representation out of these people.

We need politicians in office who are there to represent the people, not big business, unions nor any other activist group. The corruptness within politics needs to be brought to an end. It has become acceptable and expected within the political arena. Young adults are being inspired to go into politics because of the wealth to be made.

Politicians representing both parties must understand that when an individual wins an election, they are there to represent the people, including those who voted against them. I believe the political parties have lost grasp of this somewhere along the line. It is like the nation is divided into two major parties and one side is not willing to work with the other.

The old bully syndrome is kicking in on both sides of the party lines. Their mindset is it is my way or the highway. I did not vote for President Obama. I thought he did a terrible job in his first four years. I do not believe he has fulfilled his commitment to those who did vote for him in the first presidential election. And if this time around is anything like the last four years, neither side of the aisle will accomplish anything.

These grownup kids need to stop fighting and arguing. Both parties are important to this nation. Why do I say this? Because you need to work together and find some common ground to get this economy kick-started. Remember, dirty politics makes for

good headlines, but it is a bad example for our youth.

It is funny how we as parents struggle to teach our kids not to bad mouth other people. We teach them to play nice with those they come in contact with, but when it comes to politics we as parents seem to forget about all the things we have been teaching our kids.

We sit in front of the TV or radio, listen to our favorite politician representing the party we are registered under, while he or she slander other politicians in the name of winning the election.

Maybe you should consider this; set an example for your kids. The next time you hear this, reach over and turn the TV or radio off and consider this person as not being a leading example for you nor your children. And you might want to mark him or her off your list of people to vote for, because once they receive the power of their office, it is just going to get worse.

The presidential election was close this year, but there were a lot of Republicans that did not go to the polls and vote. I voted against President Obama and I cannot keep from thinking that if the Republican Party had not spent so much time on the TV and radio representing big business philosophies and bashing unions that there might have been a bigger Republican turnout at the polls. A lot of talk radio hosts seem to forget how many union members are actually registered Republicans; you know, middle class people just trying to support their families.

The reason I am writing about politics is to emphasize to parents that we need our politicians to clean up their act and become role models for our children to look up to. All the negative articles in the newspaper during elections, accusing one politician of misdoings to gain an edge and the counter article being written by the other side needs to come to a stop.

We need straight shooting politicians who are clear to the public about what they stand for, and what they will do once in office. They need to be able to get up on the stage and clearly say what they believe in and what they do not believe in.

I like listening to Donald Trump whenever he talks about politics. Yes, he is a big businessman, but he has come up with a common sense approach to kick-start this failing economy while fixing the national debt at the same time.

Trump indicated if he were in charge, he would raise the import taxes on all American company's products which are currently being produced in other countries. These products were once being assembled here in the United States and are now being assembled by workers in other countries for pennies on the dollar. The shame of the matter is they are then being shipped back to the American people to buy at high prices, as though they were assembled here in the United States.

Trump indicated this would work one of two ways; either the American companies who left under President Bill Clinton's NAFTA act would refuse to pay the tax, thus returning to the United States and reopening the many factories they closed down, or the taxes they would be forced to pay would pay off the national debt. Either way the American people win in the long run.

Trump also indicated we should be charging other countries for the cost of having our military there to protect them. Like South Korea, for instance, a prosperous country. Why is the United States footing the bill to keep our military over there? Every time the North Koreans threaten South Korea, we send the US Navy over there to patrol their waters. This is adding up to billions of American taxpayer dollars each year. Our politicians seem to think we have an endless supply of those beautiful green tax trees growing money somewhere.

There have been a number of politicians who have come forward saying we should stop foreign aid to other countries. The Democratic Senate recently voted to continue to supply foreign aid to other country's governments. The biggest part of our debt is because we are pouring hundreds of millions of dollars each month out to these foreign countries, many of which are very wealthy countries, and some of whom have made it very clear they do not like us.

This form of foreign welfare has to stop. We need to get our national debt down and we need to take care of the American people first. If there is anything left over, then we can look at helping other needy countries who deserve our support.

Folks, all of this national debt we are piling up will have to be paid off by our children in the future through higher taxes. Your hard-earned tax money is going to people who would rather kill us and our children than deal with us. It is also taking away from our household income. It's taking money away from our children's education and senior citizens who are barely getting by.

# CHAPTER 18
## JUDICIARY SYSTEM

The Judiciary system across the United States has gone through many changes over the years. Some of the changes were for the better and many for the worse. With politicians using being tough on crime as a platform for reelection and sponsoring tough on crime bills, the system has grown to be to expensive for the taxpayers to keep up with.

Tough on crime bills end up creating a lot of jobs in law enforcement and the clerical areas of various legal departments. With the new laws comes a bigger budget to support the manpower needed to enforce the letter of the law. Money must flow to those departments from the taxpayers to keep them operating.

It seems law enforcement agencies charged with monitoring today's society have become big business, because there is money to be made keeping tough on crime laws in place. There is money to be made by keeping criminals locked up.

Politician are getting elected due to the stand they take on crime. A lot of young lives are being ruined because of individuals who are in position to enforce tough on crime laws.

Some individuals enforcing these laws have lost their morals and are going too far with their power at times. They do this so their record will put them in position to receive promotions or get elected to positions. It appears sometimes these highly educated people fail to think that not all cases warrant prosecution or arrest.

Now as you know I was in law enforcement, and I will be the first to tell you, their job can be very hard at times and very rewarding at other times. But does every situation require an arrest? no! That is up to the discretion of the responding officer. Does every case have to be prosecuted? No that is up to the District Attorney's Office.

If an officer comes across a teenager who is drunk in public who has never been in trouble before, do they have to arrest them? Well, that person has broken several laws, but in the old days they would have loaded them up in the car and took them home to their parents, letting the parents know up front, if it happens again they would be coming down to the jail to visit their child.

What if your teenage son got into a fight at school over a girl? Should he be arrested or suspended? Well, a lot of high schools today have campus police who are trained to arrest people for violent acts. So in today's society a lot of times one of the two kids involved in the fight is going to be arrested for assault, which gives them a permanent criminal record.

Now I must ask you how many times have you been in a little fight at school over a girl or boy and in your mind do you feel you should have been arrested for assault? The answer is no.

Adults seem to forget what they did as kids. They seem to forget that they have a moral obligation to do the right thing when it comes to deciding another person's future. I will tell you right now, a kid who gets booked in jail for anything, their future from that point forward will be very bleak.

That booking will haunt them for the rest of their lives. It will never fall off their record. It will get them turned down for most jobs they apply for. It will turn their lives into a slow downhill spiral, which will seem impossible to climb out of. You might think

juvenile records are sealed; not these days. Most states have done away with sealing juvenile records because they have so many juvenile offenders committing adult level crimes.

In California most of our high school campuses have police officers assigned to them. This is a good thing, especially with school shootings taking place across the nation. But I do feel law enforcement should only be on campus as a visible deterrent of a serious crime. I believe there needs to be a separation between what a police officer gets involved in while working on campus and what should be taken care of by the school administration.

Even though I was employed in law enforcement for 25 years, I often wondered why all misdemeanors and some lower level felonies do not drop off a person's record after so many years. If a kid screws up, but goes five years without getting into trouble, doesn't it stand to reason after five years they should have a clean slate? This would give them the ability to get a job.

In 2006, a panel made up of three federal judges declared California's prison system overcrowded and inhumane to those it housed. They ordered the state to pour millions of dollars into the prison health system. They attached a federally appointed overseer (Receivership) to be in charge of the money and ensure the health care system was made better in the prisons.

Now a three federal judge panel made the decision to place the California prison system under receivership, ordering the state to spend millions of taxpayer dollars which were originally slated for road construction, the elderly and the K-12 school system on rapists and murders.

If they can make decisions that will bankrupt a state, than why can't they order the legal system to be overhauled and put a time period on how long certain crimes can stay on a person's criminal record?

With today's internet system in place, businesses and the everyday person can find out anything they want to know about you. Your privacy rights which once were protected by the federal government could not be violated because it was considered a felony. Now it seems the government does not care anymore and your private information is now available for anyone who is willing to pay to receive it.

They can find out about your arrest history, bankruptcy, previous addresses where you have been employed and how much money you make, how many kids you have, if you owe taxes and all the names of those in your immediate family. Now if this is not a violation of your privacy, then I do not know what is.

Personally, I do not believe employers should have access to a person's criminal record. Sure they cannot read them, but they can gather enough information to know you have committed a felony or misdemeanor. We are supposed to be trying to get those who have been in trouble with the law back into society as a productive person. But when an employer does a background check on a future employee and see that person has an arrest history, the door is immediately closed in their face.

If these guys cannot get a job then they are going to go back to what they know how to do best and that is crime. Do not take me wrong, we have career criminals out there who intend to take the easy way out and commit crimes until they take their last breath.

Another travesty in our judicial system is the plea bargaining system used throughout the country. It has placed more young people behind bars than actual trials. Some deserved it and others maintain their innocence.

A plea offer is offered to a person who is looking at being prosecuted for a crime. The D.A. will usually offer them the minimum sentence and maybe offer to drop some of the charges if they will accept a plea of guilty. The offer is usually followed by a scare tactic, indicating if the person does not accept the plea offer, he or she will be looking at the maximum sentence for the crime they are being accused of. The sentencing of the new crime can be enhanced by a individuals past criminal history.

You might say, well, if this person did not commit the crime why would they accept the plea bargain? I want to ask you something; when was the last time you were in court and watched the average public defender at work? They are overloaded with cases. I have personally seen some that looked like they slept in their suit the night before. They are not doing research on any of their cases. Most of the time, if a plea was offered to their client, they are telling them to take it. It gets one more case off of their desk.

Our legal system today is nothing like what they portray on TV shows. On TV they will usually open a show with the D.A. calling in the investigator and telling them their case has too many holes in it. It is not strong enough to prosecute and will not stand up in court.

Unfortunately, that is not how the real legal system works. I believe a lot of District Attorneys offer pleas to people with past criminal records because the case against them is not strong enough to prosecute or they are a first-time offender. So, they hope the scare tactic will work and they can walk away with a win.

While working in the prison system, I ran across a lot of inmates who took the plea because of the scare tactics. Some of these individuals said they did not commit the crime they were accused of. I also ran across a handful of inmates who did not take the plea because they said they did not commit the crime and they had a moral obligation to fight the charge. Well, as I said I ran across them in prison, so that means they lost and got the max sentence. I say do away with the plea system and only prosecute the cases that have evidence to back them up.

Our juries today do not seem to be very intelligent in regard to the letter of the law. They appear to be easily persuaded by the District Attorneys. Maybe this is because of the trend of tough on crime talks that shower our news media every day. The jury receives instructions from the judge indicating a guilty verdict must be rendered based on the evidence, and with no doubt in their minds the person is guilty.

I saw a local case where a man was found guilty of murdering his ex-wife, and there was no body found. She had just vanished. There was motive in the fact that they hated each other after their divorce.

There was not a stitch of evidence that he had actually committed murder. The D.A. based their case on theory, which as far as I know is not admissible in court. The trial received a lot of negative media coverage, and there was a lot of protest by the defense attorney on how the case was being treated within the court.

In the end a jury found this man guilty of murdering his wife on nothing more than circumstantial evidence portrayed by the District Attorney in his theories. Now I am not saying he did not do it, but I will say there was not a stitch of evidence that pointed in his

direction, and the whole case itself from day one to the end unfolded in the media in front of the public's eyes, which could not keep from tainting the jury's opinion.

The coverage by the media from the day she came up missing to the end of the trial reminded me of watching reality TV. The media was allowed to taint the minds of the public and prospective jurors. If this is what our legal system is coming to, then watch out, because we will all be looking at going to prison one day.

I say do away with the plea system and only prosecute the cases that have sound evidence to back the case. Put together a system for those who commit petty theft and drug related offenses to be placed under house arrest.

Make them go to work an pay the victim, not the state or county, five times the value of the item they took. This would save the taxpayer $50,000 a year per criminal in prison. I was once working a case upon an individual who had originally been sentenced and to a year in prison for stealing some tools out of a guy's front yard.

Eventually he was released from prison and found out his girlfriend had moved to another area not covered by his parole officer. He asked his parole officer for a transfer to the area she moved to, and was denied. His file indicated he absconded to be with her.

Eventually he was arrested and more charges were added to his time to serve. In all he was released three times from prison and absconded for one reason or another each time. Each time he was arrested and more charges were added.

This guy sat in front of me 15 years later. He had no serious charges against him except he could not follow the parole rules and he had petty theft charges. I asked him to tell me about his last arrest and what he did to get sent back to prison. He said he stole a six-pack of beer and received ten years for it.

Now I do not condone stealing, and I verified what he told me as being the truth. His reparation owed to the victim was $7.00. I cannot believe this non-violent offender, who at best I could only see had committed three petty thefts against another person, was sitting before me, and had cost the taxpayers of California over the last ten years $500,000.

I was even more surprised when I looked at his sentencing. The judge gave him ten years for the beer theft. I asked him how did that happen and he indicated the judge threw the book at him for his prior arrest for absconding.

There are a lot of cases like this sitting in prisons across the nation. I still think as a prior law enforcement officer that there has to be another method to deal with certain crimes, like house arrest and paying five to ten times the value of what was stolen back to the person the crime was committed against.

The legal system in each state has created a large financial burden on the state's budget. Our District Attorneys love a tough legal system. It means more cases for them to prosecute or plea, and more flexible avenues to convict a person utilizing the gray areas.

Let's face it, if you are a D.A. your job is to win cases. The more cases you win, the more recognition you get in the media. The more exposure the media gives you, the better chances you have of becoming a judge or a future politician. Everything in life is geared up for upward mobility.

The legal system needs to be revamped. There needs to more strict guidelines put in place by which you can prosecute an individual. The creative writing and creative thinking used to get your guy needs to be thrown out the door. Our system has opened the door for aggressive individuals with upward mobility on their minds to put many young adults who have messed up for the first time in prison.

There is a price to be paid for willful breaking the law, but where is the moral structure of the system in place? It has been filled with people taking on the role of God.

Then there is the flip side of the system that rears its ugly head, where a person who is guilty of a criminal act such as murder gets away with it because his civil rights were violated. I guess the bottom line is, your fair treatment within this legal system comes down to how good of a lawyer you can afford to hire.

Look at the O.J. Simpson trial. He was able to pay for the best attorneys. They never defended his guilt or innocence in the case. Instead they attacked the handling of the evidence and the moral background of the investigators. And he walked out with a not guilty verdict.

Believe me, I am not an activist for criminal sentencing. I am not, as we used to say in the prison system, an inmate lover. But I do feel our judicial system is not geared up the same for everybody. I believe if you are an influential person you will get leniency handed down. If you are the average Joe on the streets, you're going to get hit across the head with the book so hard it will make your head spin.

The system was not created this way, it was evolved into this by those working within it. Let's revamp the system, and get rid of the progressive sentencing for non- violent offenders.

In 1994, the Three Strikes Law was put in place in California. It was meant to be used against violent offenders, but was manipulated within the court system and utilized against non-violent offenders and even misdemeanors.

In the end, the California prison system became quickly overcrowded. It has become burdened with disgruntled inmates who are serving life sentences without the possibility of parole due to the Three Strikes Law. Some of those who were sentenced under the Three Strikes Law were struck out for committing petty theft. This misuse of the Three Strikes Law has vapor locked the legal system with appeals from lawyers and inmates indicating their clients' due process rights were violated.

After 18 years of being in place, the prison system became overcrowded and overwhelmed. The cost the taxpayer have been hit with has all but run the state into bankruptcy.

In 2012, the people of California voted to revamp the Three Strikes Law to lessen the burden on the state's financial status. It appears all offenders convicted under this law will have their cases reevaluated for possible re-sentencing.

The question I have is, why wasn't this law reviewed properly for impact on the taxpayer down the road? And why wasn't it rewritten to ensure it had no gray areas in that it could be manipulated by those in the legal system? And my final question is why was the proposition the people voted on different from what was put into law?

I guess these questions will never be answered, because politicians are what they are, and people in power a lot of the times do not look down the road for trouble that may arise, but rather live for the moment. That is why I put this chapter in the book, not because it helps you raise your child, but rather I hope it will make you more aware of how you vote. Remember, the politicians we elect into office, can have a very big

impact on your child's future.

# CHAPTER 19
## PRISON SYSTEM

As parents, next to dying, your young adult going to prison is probably the worst thing that can
happen to you and them. It means one of two
things, either you as a parent failed to raise your
child properly, or your child refused to follow your
teachings and advice growing up.

It's important that you take an active role in
your child's life, because if you do not, I guarantee a negative influence will. Monitor what they
watch on TV, as well as the video games they
play. You cannot shelter your children from society, but you can give them proper guidance while
raising them guidance that teaches them right
from wrong.

If you have a teenager with a track record of
getting into trouble with the law, their final des-
tination will be prison if they do not correct their
behavior issues. At some point the judicial system
will get tired of giving them breaks, resulting in
them being placed in some type of lockup setting.

Even though you have tried every avenue to get
it across to your child, they still ended up behind
bars. It is normal for a parent to feel guilt, anger
and embarrassment. But I want you to know if
you did everything in your power to straighten

them out, then guilt is not warranted.

The next feeling you will probably have is that law enforcement is picking on your child. Let's get something straight, the local police are not sitting outside your door waiting on little Johnny to go hell bent on a binge of destruction. Your child found themselves behind bars due to bad decision making and a lack of respect for you, because they refused to listen to what you were telling them.

When you have a child that is constantly defying authority, and the laws of society, they will give you only half truths as to why they are in trouble. They want your protection when they need it, and a person on their side. They also feel a certain amount of embarrassment about letting you down once again. And finally they need allies fighting for them, who are kept partially in the dark.

This type of behavior never stops with a reckless mind. Even while working in prison, I saw this personality over and over. Inmates who got in trouble with the correctional staff or other inmates would call or write home to those they felt they had been buffaloed through the years, trying to convince them they are being picked on again.

Unfortunately, they never told the person who was being kept in the dark that they spit in an officer's face or they ran up a huge drug debt with other inmates on the yard. The best thing you can do with a youth who gets into trouble with authority figures is let them know up front you are not buying their poor excuse nor the half truths they are telling you.

The next thing you need to reassure them of is that you do love them. Let them know you are there to help them, not get them out of trouble, but to support them in making the right decisions that will stop them from having conflicts with the law.

You will also have to assure them it is their responsibility to help themselves by stopping the behavior that is getting them into trouble. Do not become an enabler to them, someone they can count on to spend money to get them out of a bad situation.

When a parent constantly bails a kid out of trouble, the only lesson they learn is you will be there to clean up after each mess they get into. At some point tough love has to kick in, because they are looking at your kindness as weakness.

To help your child the first thing you as a parent need to do is figure out what is causing them to get into trouble. Is it the people they have chose to associate with, or is it a drug related issue? You have to find the root of the problem. Once you find that, then you will have an angle to attack the issue.

If it is the people they socialize with, then detach them from those people. Make those individuals very uncomfortable about being in your child's company. I am sure by now you have become acquainted with a police officer or two who has dealt with your child on more than one occasion.

Let the officer know who the bad influence is, and let him have a talk with these people. If your child is bringing too much heat on them, they won't want him or her around. You can also try the military route. Catch your young adult when they are very scared and get them signed up for the military. Find a recruiter who can get them out of town fast.

The reason I say the military is because they will offer a structured environment for your child. They will also basically brainwash them by stripping their old ways of thinking away, and replace it with the military way. Back in the '60s and '70s the military helped a lot of troubled youth straighten out their lives.

Back in the old days when you constantly got in trouble with the law, it would finally come down to a judge asking you if you would rather go to prison or would like to enlist in the military. Those practices went to the wayside when the military started downsizing and became more selective in who they enlisted.

Let's talk about the waste of a person's life spent in prison. Let me give you a little guided tour of my 25 years working the maximum security units to the general population main lines. Let's start off by saying most prison terms given to inmates are in some way drug related, whether it be rape, murder or theft while under the influence.

for about 50% of the inmate population, prison is their home, a safe haven from the realities of life. These types of people have spent the better part of their lives in some type of lockup unit, whether it is a boys ranch, juvenile hall, county jail or youth authority. I say this because at least 50% of the inmate population is institutionalized. Prison is the only home they know that make them feel comfortable.

The time they spend on the streets with their families is just considered a vacation from the normal prison life they live. Most of them are granted parole with no intention of staying out of prison. They just want to go home, get high, drink, and catch up on old times with a few friends, then commit a crime to go back to their normal prison life. As sad as it sounds, this is their reality.

We actually have inmates who intentionally commit a minor assault on staff the day they are supposed to be released on parole to keep from going back to the streets. These types of inmates are usually the people who spent most of their lives as homeless people living on the streets.

When they go to prison they have a far better life than when they lived on the streets. They get three meals a day, free medical care, much better than what most elderly get on the streets. They have a warm bed and live in a climate controlled environment, with hot showers. They only have to get out of bed if they want to eat or if they are assigned a job.

When they go to the exercise yard, they meet up with old friends who spend the day with them talking about crimes they committed in the past. If they want exercise they play soccer, handball, softball and even horseshoes all day long. Outside of being confined to their area and not allowed to leave when they want, "They live the life of Riley."

Inmates come from all walks of life, from being third generation gang members to being raised with a silver spoon in their mouths. All in all, prison is a collection of the biggest misfits society could produce. It is a collection of murderers, gang members, thieves of all types, drug addicts/

alcoholics, rapists, child molesters and also the aggressive mentally ill.

Does prison rehabilitate a person's mentality? No. Rehabilitation can only start from within by admitting to guilt. Over my years working in prison, I only came across three inmates that admitted to doing the crime they committed. These three were genuinely sorry for the crime they committed and the lives they destroyed along the way, and would be the first to tell you they belong in prison.

Prison does not rehabilitate an inmate's mind, but it does reshape their mentality by educating them to be a better criminal and making them harder inside. The education they receive about how to be a better criminal comes from talking to other criminals about where they went wrong in the crime they committed. They utilize the information they gather to perfect their next planned crime, which they believe they will not get caught committing.

You cannot reform a person from a life of crime in the manner educated people think. These are not common people, but rather streetwise hardened criminals who taught themselves survival techniques. The only way to reform a criminal from going back to prison is to make prison so harsh and unbearable they would rather die than be there.

I once asked an inmate why he kept selling drugs and coming back to prison. I told him he needed to straighten his life out and get a normal job. He looked at me and then laughed, replying, "Officer Shaw, you work hard to earn $4,000 a month. I only work a few hours a night and in a good night I can bring in $5,000 easy." I then asked him, "Don't you get tired of being locked up in prison?" He replied, "Don't you get tired of barely making your bills each month?" He went on to tell me prison was a small price to pay because he had thousands of dollars stashed in bank accounts and when he hit his goal he would retire from crime.

All these educated people and bureaucrats think the road to reform is through educating inmates. I say they are full of it. You have to remember you are dealing with people who could have had an education if they wanted it, but instead they chose to skip school and hang out with the criminal element.

Inmates could care less about education while in prison, unless it meant they had a shot at getting out early. Their motive for attending school is not about getting educated, but about getting an early release.

The prison system needs to be designed in a military boot camp fashion. They need to be stripped of their old ways and brainwashed into new ways of thinking, just as the military does to new recruits. Some need to do hard labor, something they are not use to doing on the streets.

The prison environment needs to be miserable to the point that they never want to come back, and the bleeding hearts need to be silenced because they are in the way of true rehabilitation. Their own agendas of making money off of the inmates has gotten in the way of progress. When this takes place within the prison system in California or any other state, then and only then will the return rate slow down and reform kick in.0

Prisons in California are not set up to persuade an individual from wanting to return. They are nothing more than a warehouse or resort. There are too many bleeding heart activists who, believe it or not, want these guys locked up. But they want their environment to be as though the inmate is staying at a resort on vacation.

Why do these bleeding hearts want criminals locked up? Well, it's simple. They want to ensure their families are safe and there are a lot of them making money on the streets by representing these criminals in court litigation against the state.

It's funny. There are very few times an inmate actually wins a lawsuit against the state prison system, but the activist lawyers representing them get a healthy payday from the state every quarter. See, inmates do not pay for their own lawyers, the people of California pay for it quarterly.

While working in the prison system, I had a chance to see so many different types of personalities locked up with mental illness. These personality traits ranged from the severe passive, who allowed everyone to walk on them, to the master manipulator who was constantly on the con. Then you have the inmate who possesses the animal like behavior, pacing back and forth in their cells waiting to pounce on someone. Do not forget about the serial killer, who seems to be always in his element and in full control of his environment.

The one thing I noticed about serial killers is they never show remorse for their victims. Matter of fact, they are usually proud of what they have accomplished. They seem to have the attitude that if their victims were stupid enough to fall into their traps then they deserved to die. They also put on the personality trait of thinking they are more intelligent than anyone else surrounding them. Once imprisoned they love the attention they receive from the media, as though it was a reward for their hard work.

Since the state saw fit to close down almost all of the state hospitals in the late 1980s, the prison system has become overwhelmed by the criminally insane.

I once had an inmate who was mentally ill and had a split personality. He was always smiling and very talkative, but all it took was a trigger word and he would turn violent quickly. The trigger was never the same. One minute you were having a conversation with a smiling individual and the next minute you were wrestling him to the ground.

Even though I feel the mental health industry has become a big business in this country, we definitely need it. With the impact the entertainment industry has had on our children's minds, they have become very prone to violence, hardened inside with no remorse for their actions, and in some cases mentally ill.

Their minds are being altered by their environment and sometimes they are misled into a different reality other than the one most of us live in. There are various young groups popping up across the nation, such as Goths, Tagger crews and even gangs themselves.

These groups are tugging away at your children's fascination, offering them the things you have said no to. There objective is to grow in number and become powerful through intimidation. They get the group's name out to prospective members by word of mouth, so they can make their own mark in society. For most of these groups the more negative their name is the better they like it.

I have had many opportunities to be in the company of different types of mentally ill and criminally insane people. On the other hand, I have also come in contact with many more inmates, who were faking mental illness. They put on this charade to try to keep from being held accountable for their actions, as well as to keep other inmates at a distance.

There is a class of criminals who play on societal sympathy for leniency for the crimes they have committed. There is one thing I can tell you about criminals. Most of them are very intelligent and very creative. Their minds are always working on their next big criminal act the job they know in their hearts they will not get caught doing.

They are well versed on the laws governing punishment. By being in the company of other criminals they have found out what works to get leniency and what does not. They fully understand if they can portray they were not of a sound mind during the committing of their crime, they may avoid trial or perhaps get a lesser sentence if found guilty.

The difference between a person who is righteously mentally ill and one who is not is the mentally ill person tries very hard to look and act like a normal person, and does not understand they are not pulling it off.

A criminal who is pretending to be mentally ill, in an attempt to make other people believe they are emotionally unstable, cannot keep the act up 24/7 without letting their guard down every once in a while.

Criminals have learned over the years from each other how to work the justice system. When a person commits murder, the first thing a judge will do is have them examined by a psychiatrist to see if they are mentally fit to stand trial. Criminals have educated themselves over the years on how to act and answer the psychiatrist's questions properly, in an attempt to show they are incompetent to stand trial. Most of the time these attempts fail.

I once was around an inmate in an infirmary setting in max security. The inmate was in fear for his life. He summoned staff, saying that he was having a medical problem, and collapsed to the ground upon their arrival. He immediately went into a comatose state and was unresponsive. His vitals were fine, except he was unresponsive.

This inmate spent two months in the infirmary being fed through an I.V. tube. The doctors indicated all along he was not in a coma. He was prodded and poked and never flinched. Two months down the road his parole date came around. His counselor went onto the tier and spoke out loud indicating, "I guess John Doe will not be able to parole to the streets. He will have to go to a state hospital." The next thing you know he rises up like the living dead, and starts yelling, "What am I doing in here?"

I told this story to show you how good and trained criminals are at what they do. Their manipulation tactics and their ability to put mind over matter to obtain their goal is unreal.

Criminals today are very educated in the career field they have chosen, Crime. Mental health care professionals have not helped the situation by taking on the attitude of a mentally ill person is not responsible for their actions.

I have a psychiatrist friend who once told me his colleagues feel sympathy for mentally ill patients to the point they do not hold them accountable for their actions. There have been many cases where mentally ill patients in state hospitals have seriously hurt or killed health care professionals and were not prosecuted because they were protected by the umbrella of not being responsible for their actions.

This doctor friend of mine said murder is a calculated act, not a random act. It is a planned action by some mentally ill people being detained in a controlled environment. The plan is kept deep in the back of their mind, waiting for the perfect opportunity to execute it. He said these types of mentally ill people thrive on violent acts. It excites them and the only way to stop it from happening again is to execute them.

In the prison system psychiatrist use many types of mind altering drugs to treat violent mentally ill inmates. Most of these drugs slow down the thought process, and relax the inmate to the point of being very lethargic. I did not meet many inmates who went through this process who did not try to resist the treatment by refusing to take their medication. Most of them did not like the way it took their control away from them.

The only problem with utilizing mind altering medications to control a person's aggressiveness, is once they stop taking it their true violent side returns very quickly. Drug treatment is not a permanent cure, it is just a band-aid.

When a mentally ill inmate paroles to the streets, they have a habit of refusing to continue their medication. Once off their medication their aggressive side returns very quickly, and all the predatory thoughts they had harbored in the back of their mind may come out and be acted on.

I have little faith in the drug and alcohol programs within the prison system. It is hard to rehabilitate a drug addict when medical doctors are giving them painkillers, such as Vicodin and Morphine like it is candy. I truly believe most of these drug programs, especially within the prison system, are nothing more than corporate "get rich" schemes.

There are so many businesses out there who feed off of laws put in place by states. They see it as a way to get rich fast. Results are not a major issue with them unless they are about to lose their contract. Then all of a sudden they put together some phony statistics on how well they are doing, or they may not even worry about good statistics at all, because they have already made the money they intended to and it is time for them to get out of Dodge.

The mental health industry has become a big business in this country and it is certainly a big business in the California Prison System. The medical industry is no different than any other big business. They will say and do whatever it takes to make money. That's their bottom line.

You see that when you go to the hospital and your bill indicates they charged your insurance company $200 for a band-aid.

In California the medical industry in the prison system as well as the welfare system has grown out of control. Prisons themselves were never designed to be mental asylums. The cost of retrofitting the prisons with mental health staff is breaking the state.

Inmate lawyers are breaking the state, and now attacking the county jails with the same pressure tactics they went after the State Prison System with. Federal Judges are making rulings in California that are not in line with other state's prison systems.

This is happening because California has an inmate Bill of Rights and most other states do not. This Bill of Rights has been breaking the backs of the California taxpayers for years, and has resulted in the criminals who have abused their bodies with drugs for years getting better medical treatment than those on the streets.

Because of lawsuits filed by prison activists, a three judge federal panel, declared California's prison system was overcrowded and inhumane to those it housed. They ordered the State to pour millions of dollars into the prison health system. They attached a federal appointed overseer (receivership) to be in charge of the money and ensure the health care system was made better in the system.

The first receiver who the federal judges put in place awarded himself a salary of $500,000 a year and his hand-picked assistants received $300,000 a year each. He also went on to wine and dine people and had a good time on taxpayer's money to the tune of $400,000. Once the judges found out what he had been doing they ordered him to pay it back and fired him.

I am going to let you know right now there was nothing wrong with the health care system the prison system had in place. Yes, it was undermanned, and those working in it had been asking for more personnel for a very long time. But proper medical attention was being received. Those who were faking illness for reasons of attaining a future lawsuit against the state or because they were drug addicts trying to get a fix were weeded out.

Those who were truly ill got all the help they needed. Over time, those inmates who were being manipulative filed complaints with activist attorneys who managed to get their issues heard by the federal judicial system.

In the end the receivership was born and all it did was almost bankrupt the state of California. The prison medical system is now filled with nurses who have a lack of job related experience and have no interaction skills. The inmates who truly need medical attention have been pushed to the back of the line by all those who are trying to manipulate the system.

The inmate population will tell you they want the old system back. They feel like they were dealing with staff that were more professional at that time, and who cared about their needs.

I do not know how the federal judicial system thinks it has the authority to place a state under receivership. They knew without a doubt this decision would place the state's budget under tremendous hardship. Under the receivership billions of taxpayer's dollars were poured into the medical industry's pockets. In the end money desperately needed elsewhere in the state was not available for proper use.

They based their decision on inmates dying daily in all the various prisons in California, which they deemed to be malpractice. These prisons are like little cities within the city you live in. Do people not die at home or in the hospital every day?

A lot of these deaths were inmates who were well into the geriatric stage of life. I sat in on several autopsies in my career and most of the inmates who died from normal causes died from blown out arteries due to their past drug addiction.

A weak artery caused by many years of drug abuse is not detectable. One minute it is working fine and the next minute it blows out and the person is dead. This is not unlike the hundreds of people who die annually in society from aneurysms. All in all these deaths should not have been labeled malpractice. It was just a catchy term used by lawyers to get the judge's attention.

Let's talk about the overcrowding a little more. Yes, California's prison system is without a doubt overcrowded. The return rate of criminals is off the chart. Inmates do not fear coming back to prison because there is no deterrent. Life for most inmates in prison is easier than life on the streets.

California has a huge amount of lifers due to the Three Strikes Law. We also have a large population of lifers who have committed murder and have been incarcerated for 20 years or more. There are lifers within the system that had committed murder in their younger years who I feel would be good candidates for release.

They have served 15 to 25 years behind bars, without getting into trouble. Most of them are old gang members who are no longer active and committed their crime against a rival gang member. I feel these types of inmates who have a paper trail indicating they have been a model inmate should be given a release date. These are not mentally ill people nor serial killers. They are inmates who killed other rival gang members as kids or young adults.

We have what we call the Board of Prison Terms. This is a group of people who evaluate an individual and determine if they are a good candidate for release. More times than not when an inmate goes before the board they are turned down. I believe this happens not because the inmate is not a good candidate for release, but because no one wants to be the one who released a murderer who may murder again.

Before I retired there was an old man in a wheelchair on the yard I worked on. He was at least 80 years old. He was in prison because he killed his wife's lover, whom he caught her in bed with. This old man had been in prison since the 1970s. He was confined to a wheelchair, spending his whole day on the yard sleeping. For the life of me, I cannot believe he had not been released from prison long ago.

The BPT within the prison system needs to step up and do their job. Yes, we all would like to play it safe and not make any decisions in life that may fail or jeopardize our career, but that's not what they get paid for. They get paid to evaluate an inmate for possible release, and if their record indicates they have been a model inmate for 20 years then give them a date.

Let's talk about one of the most controversial subjects that exists within the prison system, the death sentence. I will start off by saying, I am a full supporter of the death penalty. But I am not a supporter of the current red tape filled system in California that has only allowed 13 convicted criminals to be executed since 1978.

My opinion is, if we are going to have such a law in place then let's line them up and start using it. So far the death penalty in California is nothing more than a taxpayer burden, which has made a stable living for activist lawyers sitting outside of San Quentin Prison.

Currently California has 729 inmates sitting on death row. The average cost of each death row inmate is costing the taxpayers approximately $100,000 a year. The cost is double compared to a non-death row inmate, who costs the taxpayers an average of $50,000 per year.

It is said through various studies that the death sentence law costs the taxpayers an average of $180,000,000 per year. That's a lot of school supplies for our children, or more teachers so the classrooms can have fewer students. The money could also be put toward better roads and lowering taxes. I believe many people in the federal judicial system are very liberal minded, and the death penalty will always be held up for one thing or another, meaning no convicted felons will be executed.

Since 1978 we have had 57 death row inmates die from natural causes. That number is more than triple the number who have died from execution. There were 20 suicides since 1978 on death row and the suicide number is even higher than those actually executed. I have to ask myself as a taxpayer, is the death penalty worth the bang for my buck? Or would life in prison without possibility of parole be a better alternative at a cost of $50,000 a year per inmate, versus what it is costing at this present time?

If the death penalty was abolished it would immediately save the taxpayers $180 million per year and $5 billion over 20 years. That is a lot of money that could go back toward our children. Fifty percent of the cost to house a death row inmate is their legal cost, which is paid for by the California taxpayer.

The prison system is a huge financial burden on the state. The people that work there work with their hands tied 90% of the time. Lawyers on both the state side and the inmate side of the aisle have mucked up the system so bad that I foresee all inmates will have to be confined to their cells to keep from violating their rights.

Lawsuit settlements coming down from the federal level in regard to the medical

system has bogged down the system so badly that it is almost impossible to function at the custodial level, resulting in morale being at an all time low for custodial staff and inmates alike.

The current system needs to be cleaned up of this bogged down mess created by lawyers, who have the goal of just making money. There are at least five medical lawsuits covering mental health and disabilities that need to be refined into one operational policy. In its current state of affairs the employees working within the prison system cannot uphold one category of inmate rights without violating another category of their rights.

In all the taxpayers have been burdened for years by both lawyers with ambitions to make money off the state by representing inmates, and the Democrats who have supported a huge free handout system (welfare) with the objective to control the votes in the major metropolitan areas. Between the exceptional medical care system put in place in the prison system and the free handout system in the state of California, the state has all but gone broke.

The politicians have offset the state budget downfalls by going after fast money, cutting school budgets, cutting all state employee wages except those who directly work for the politicians themselves by 25%, and raising taxes.

Is there anything that can be done to offset the cost of operating the prison system? Yes, first of all go back to the old medical system that was in place. Stop giving known addicts painkillers to feed their drug addiction. Put the inmates to work to offset their upkeep.

If I were in charge of the prison operations, I would make it more self sufficient. You would have to change some laws that would allow corporate business to come inside the prison walls to set up shop in a building that already exists.

These corporate businesses could employ inmates at a lesser hourly rate than on the streets. They could pay inmates a minimum wage of $5.00 hour. The inmate would pocket $2 per hour, his victim restitution would get $2 of his hourly wage, and the state would get $1.

In addition, the state could charge the business $50 for each large item produced, such as furniture, or $50 per boxed item that left the assembly line. This would offset prison budget burden for the state and taxpayers. The inmates would be very happy, because jobs that pay $2 hour in the prison are unheard of.

It would benefit the businesses by reducing their overhead greatly because their employees already have medical coverage. The state is already paying the electric bill and the buildings already exist.

All in all there is a lot of work that needs to be done to clean up the burden the taxpayers have been given. As I have shown you, prison is not a good alternative for your young adult, if you can keep that from happening. Monitor your children growing up, and instill a sense of right from wrong. Start at a very early age, teaching them about what type of friends they want to be associated with, and hopefully your hard work will pay off.

Lightning Source UK Ltd.
Milton Keynes UK
UKOW06f0332031116
286741UK00022B/525/P